The How-to Guide for

Integrating the
Common
Core in
Language
Arts

Authors
Debby Murphy
Wendy Conklin

Foreword
Debi Crimmins, Ph.D.

SHELL EDUCATION

Publishing Credits

Robin Erickson, *Production Director;* Lee Aucoin, *Creative Director;*
Timothy J. Bradley, *Illustration Manager;* Sara Johnson, M.S.Ed., *Editorial Director;*
Jennifer Viñas, *Editor;* Lori Nash, M.S.Ed., *Editor;* Sara Sciuto, *Assistant Editor;*
Grace Alba Le, *Designer;* Corinne Burton, M.A.Ed., *Publisher*

Shell Education

5301 Oceanus Drive
Huntington Beach, CA 92649-1030
http://www.shelleducation.com

ISBN 978-1-4258-1311-6

© 2014 Shell Educational Publishing, Inc.

Integrating the Common Core in Language Arts

Table of Contents

Foreword. 5

Acknowledgements 7

Chapter 1: Empowering Teachers. 9

Chapter 2: Navigating the CCSS 15

Chapter 3: Selecting Text That Works. 33

Chapter 4: Identifying Higher-Order Thinking Within the CCSS 57

Chapter 5: Close Reading in the Classroom 93

Chapter 6: *I Do* and *We Do*—Modeled and Shared
    Interactive Strategy Use. 115

Chapter 7: Moving into Small Instructional Groups:
    You Try—Guided Strategy Use 131

Chapter 8: Independent Reading:
    You Do—Independent Strategy Use 159

Chapter 9: Writing Through the Lens of the CCSS. 175

Chapter 10: Bringing It All Together 197

Appendix A: Teacher Resources 212

Appendix B: References Cited 216

Foreword

Have you ever found yourself lost while driving in your car—perhaps on some ominous, dark highway that you exited on to by total accident, or in a rental car in a strange city where you have no idea of the complicated road layout? Perhaps you're just one of those people that has no ego issue in admitting that you are just everyday "directionally challenged." Then, somehow miraculously, the navigational GPS kicks on, quiets your fears, and it "talks you in?" It is a powerfully calming experience when you get the sense of, "I'm going to be ok, and I know where I'm heading now. Thank you GPS." That is exactly what I experienced when I read Debby Murphy and Wendy Conklin's *The How-to Guide for Integrating the Common Core in Language Arts*. Welcome to safe travels, as this will become your new GPS for successfully navigating the implementation of the Common Core State Standards into all language arts as well as content-area classrooms.

This book is going to sound very close to home if you are an educator who has heard so much about the CCSS, and simultaneously wondered how in the world am I supposed to integrate these standards into what I thought I already was supposed to teach. In fact, we are all aware by now that the CCSS lay out a "rigorous literacy journey for students, as well as teachers, on skills and deep understandings for college and career readiness." Debby Murphy and Wendy Conklin provide an undeniable "roadmap," for even the most hesitant of Common Core "drivers," as they beautifully provide ready-to-use application strategies for not only all teachers, but for all levels of students, as well.

From the very first page, this resource provides its readers with that validating language that empowers all teachers as they travel down the Common Core pathway. The authors confirm the importance of CCSS being the *what* for literacy learning, with specific expectations for all students at all grade levels. More importantly, they take our CCSS navigation to the next level as they advocate the importance of all teachers being the *how* to the Common Core journey, and extending that *how* with students—*how* the reading and writing strategies look, *how* to do the strategies, and ultimately *how* to apply the standards. The text is laid out in a way that finally demystifies the step-by-step route that teachers can use for applying the standards.

The beauty of this book is that it seamlessly helps all teachers, new and experienced, travel through "intentional decisions" for implementing CCSS within the classroom. Teachers will learn specific thought provoking strategies for easily adding CCSS standards to daily literacy instruction. From unpacking the mechanics of the standards, to selecting the right reading to build text complexity, to promoting deep, close reading, to identifying higher-order thinking skills that apply all depths of knowledge, to writing in response to reading with text-dependent evidence—*Integrating the Common Core in Language Arts* is definitely the book that pulls it all together in a way that is insightful, real, and full of a genuine understanding of the students, classrooms, and literacy. Debby Murphy and Wendy Conklin know kids, they know reading, and they know how to make sense of the Common Core. With their expert guidance, we will all undoubtedly find a successful destination with implementing the CCSS into every classroom. Congratulations in selecting this resource as your roadmap. You have arrived!

—Debi Crimmins, Ph.D.
Former Associate Superintendent of Curriculum and Instruction,
Area South,
Orlando, Florida

Acknowledgements

We would like to acknowledge the contributions of the many individuals whose work helped to solidify the writing of this book. We would like to express our appreciation specifically to Lisa Callahan, Karie Gladis, and Kimberly O'Connor-Stockton for their valuable notes, ideas, and work from their professional development presentations. Their work is the foundation and structure found in Chapter 2, Navigating the CCSS, as well as many key parts of Chapter 3, Selecting Text That Works.

Debby thanks Wendy Conklin for her encouragement as her co-author and friend. She also gratefully acknowledges the love and support of her husband, Mike. She is blessed by her grandchildren, Henry and Katherine, who continually remind her of the importance of the future of education and draw her once again into the magic of learning to read.

Wendy thanks her girls, Raegan and Jordan, and her husband Blane, who have served as partners in writing as they listened, brainstormed, and offered ideas as well as samples for this book. And no one knows this better . . . this book could not have been written without the support and expertise of Debby, one of the best literacy experts Wendy knows.

Chapter

Empowering Teachers

> *We have to be continually jumping off cliffs and developing our wings on the way down.*
>
> —Kurt Vonnegut

Perhaps the implementation of the Common Core State Standards (CCSS) in your district has not caused a rise in teachers' lounge therapy sessions, partial hair loss, or extreme caffeine consumption. But the truth of the matter is that these standards have caused many good teachers to lose some much needed sleep as they wonder: *How do I integrate these standards into what I already thought I was supposed to teach? Do we have to develop a new curriculum? How do I go about really understanding how to implement these standards with my students? What should I do to make sure that my students are successful?*

The Common Core State Standards for English Language Arts & Literacy in History/Social Studies, Science, and Technical Subjects lay out a rigorous literacy journey for students by articulating the skills and understandings that students need for college and career readiness in multiple disciplines. "As a natural outgrowth of meeting the charge to define college and career readiness, the standards also lay out a vision of what it means to be a literate person in the twenty-first century. Indeed, the skills and understandings students are expected to demonstrate have wide applicability outside the classroom or workplace" (CCSS, http://www.corestandards.org/ELA-Literacy). At this point in implementation of the ELA Common Core State Standards in your state, you have all probably been part of professional learning to "unpack" the standards—the thinking behind the CCSS, the organization of the CCSS, what the standards say for your grade level. If you are still a bit fuzzy on all of this material, see Chapter 2 for a good review. But before we begin, it is essential that we understand the CCSS and what we need to teach our students.

The CCSS, as stated, provide educators the *what* for literacy learning. Laid out before them, teachers see clear, specific expectations for their grade level. Teachers are also encouraged to examine the standards vertically in order to understand the breadth and range of how the standards evolve. But the CCSS do not provide the *how* for us. We have the latitude in the CCSS to design instruction that effectively addresses where our students are as learners and to differentiate that instruction toward the standards based on their strengths and needs (2010, 4). In this book, as you reflect on the *how* of CCSS implementation, you will find ideas and strategies that you can really use day to day in your classroom. As you read, we pledge to be both your cheerleaders and your coaches as we explore the possibilities of the *how* together.

> We have the latitude in the CCSS to design instruction that effectively addresses where our students are as learners and to differentiate that instruction toward the Standards based on their strengths and needs. In this book, as you reflect on the how of CCSS implementation, you will find ideas and strategies that you can really use day to day in your classroom.

The most significant piece for students as they take on the high expectations of the standards is you! Many experts recognize that a strong, effective teacher is the key for student achievement—more than any specific curriculum or program (Allington and Johnston 2001; Darling-Hammond 1999; Duffy 1997). After observing multiple teachers from six states in actual instructional contexts, Richard Allington (2002) concludes unequivocally that "expertise matters." Your content understanding, your instructional decisions, and your relationships with students frame that expertise.

We recognize that exemplary teachers are crucial to the implementation of the CCSS. Their choices in the *how* ensure that students learn. These teachers know that powerful instruction takes time—long blocks of time for students to actually engage in reading and writing and speaking and listening. They plan for extensive experiences with text where students engage actively and repeatedly in authentic contexts with the strategies and skills called for in the standards. They design meaningful literacy tasks in which students interact with text and their peers. The teachers embed literacy throughout the school day, and they recognize that reading and writing are essential tools during content-area learning as well. We have several examples within the chapters of this book from real teacher experts who can show you how they accomplished this integrated literacy learning.

Along with other expert teachers, we believe that strong instruction begins with sharing the *how* with students—how the strategy looks, how to do the strategy, how to apply the standard. We craft explicit models and demonstrations to bring new learning forward. We demonstrate the *how* through significant, carefully orchestrated experiences with text. The CCSS are all about text; high expectations are set forth for students to deeply comprehend grade-level complex text. The expert teacher provides students with a plethora of text, from both literary and informational texts, for students to read across the curriculum. We show you how to move from close reading of a text to modeled lessons with text, from small instructional groups to independent reading, immersing your students in "just right" text as well as in text experiences that challenge them at the cusp of their ability.

The heart and soul of the CCSS rest in students thoughtfully engaging with text and carefully uncovering the layers of meaning in text. We see teachers who are masters at weaving provocative questions into academic discourse about texts and students who respond eagerly. Yet we also find that many teachers need a framework to get them started to ensure that they ask rigorous, thought-provoking, and text-dependent questions that send students back into the text to support and defend their thinking and claims. Many standards call for this higher-order thinking, and we show you how to ask questions that will stimulate students' thinking and move

> *Along with other expert teachers, we believe that strong instruction begins with sharing the "how" with students—how the strategy looks, how to do the strategy, how to apply the standard. We craft explicit models and demonstrations to bring new learning forward. We demonstrate the how through significant, carefully orchestrated experiences with text.*

them into engaging conversations about text with the goal that the students eventually take over and ask those higher-order questions themselves. These types of questions support metacognition (students thinking about their thinking) and promote 21st century skills with which students analyze and evaluate a wide variety of texts, including multimodal sources.

Not only do students respond to reading through speaking and listening, but, as emphasized in the CCSS, they must also use writing as a tool to share their thinking. Expert teachers set aside time in the instructional day to teach the art of writing and give their students time to write. We provide a chapter to help you consider the *how* of meeting these CCSS writing expectations as your students learn to compose narrative, informational, and opinion/ argument texts.

Overall, our goal is to support you as you make intentional decisions about how to implement the CCSS in your classroom. We believe in you as teachers, in your personal expertise and commitment to your students. We know that we can all construct a context where students flourish as learners. Within this book, we offer you multiple ideas and resources to help you be intentional as you design and differentiate instruction for your students. We provide a variety of choices to enhance your teaching as you dive into the CCSS. As you unwrap the gift of the *what*—the CCSS—you choose the best *how* to craft instruction that fosters student success.

As you peruse this book, you can, of course, read it in any order that best fits your needs. However, we would strongly suggest that you do read Chapters 6, 7, and 8 consecutively, as the content flows together. The following information provides a brief overview of what you will find in each chapter.

Chapter 2, *Navigating the CCSS*, introduces the structure of the standards for those who might need a refresher on how the standards are organized.

Chapter 3, *Selecting Text That Works*, explains what text complexity really means so teachers can discern the correct text levels for students as they match text to readers. Teachers will also discover how to put together strong text sets for the classroom that are multileveled, multimodal, and multigenre.

Chapter 4, *Identifying Higher-Order Thinking Within the CCSS*, aligns higher-order thinking questions to the CCSS Anchor Standards. We demonstrate how to use an effective framework for writing questions and designing performance tasks that meet the standard's level of rigor.

Chapter 5, *Close Reading in the Classroom*, explains how teachers can lead students through a sustained, in-depth examination of short complex texts through higher-order thinking questions. Through multiple reads, the students learn to uncover the layers of meaning within the text, with the goal that the students will carry this expertise into their own independent reading.

Chapter 6, *"I Do" and "We Do"—Modeled and Shared Interactive Strategy Use*, helps teachers design targeted model lessons, demonstrations, and examples of the strategies/skills encompassed by the CCSS. We clearly show the progression of the *I Do* lesson into interactive practice where students begin to try on the strategy/skill in a shared context.

Chapter 7, *Moving into Small Instructional Groups: "You Try"—Guided Strategy Use*, describes the focused, guided context that small groups provide and shows how teachers can use these instructional groups as an integral part of bringing students to the expectation of reading and deeply comprehending grade-level complex texts.

Chapter 8, *Independent Reading: "You Do"—Independent Strategy Use*, explicitly outlines how you can support your students through the gradual release of responsibility as they take on the ownership of the CCSS in their own independent reading.

Chapter 9, *Writing Through the Lens of the CCSS*, outlines a powerful writing process that gives teachers the time and opportunity necessary for students to plan, compose, revise, edit, and publish the three types of writing called for in the CCSS.

Chapter 10, *Bringing It All Together*, provides several integrated examples that illustrate how teachers seamlessly and intentionally weave multiple standards into authentic learning contexts that encompass both ELA and content-area learning. The lessons effectively weave together many of the ideas and strategies presented throughout this book.

Chapter 2

Navigating the CCSS

> *The Common Core State Standards provide a consistent, clear understanding of what students are expected to learn, so teachers and parents know what they need to do to help them. The standards are designed to be robust and relevant to the real world, reflecting the knowledge and skills that our young people need for success in college and careers. With American students fully prepared for the future, our communities will be best positioned to compete successfully in the global economy.*
> —Common Core State Standards Initiative, Mission Statement

The Common Core State Standards provide a consistent, clear understanding of what students are expected to learn at each grade level so that teachers can effectively design targeted, powerful instruction, thus ensuring that students achieve those standards. The standards are written to be robust and relevant to the real world, reflecting the knowledge and skills that our young people need for later success in college and careers.

Many people are at different places in their Common Core journey. Some are just becoming aware of these standards, while other districts are analyzing crosswalk documents to see how the standards they have used in the past align with the CCSS. Teachers are busy "unpacking" the standards to understand what students need to know and be able to do. District coordinators are busy creating pacing guides and benchmark assessments. Directors of curriculum and instruction are mapping curriculum resources to incorporate the standards, while teachers are considering the teaching and learning shift essential to master the CCSS. As the authors of the standards have stated in many ways, the CCSS provide the *what* to teach, but school districts and teachers will determine the *how* for successfully implementing and instructing with these standards.

Figure 2.1 Implementing the CCSS

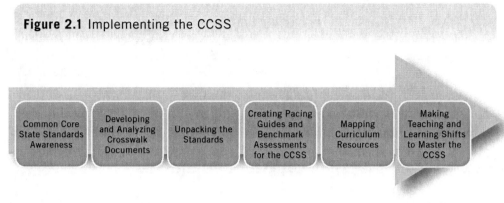

(adapted from Gladis 2013, slide 9)

Where is your school on this continuum of implementation? If you are new to understanding the CCSS and are wondering how to navigate them, this chapter is for you. We will discuss how the standards are organized, as well as the learning progressions, and finally examine how to unpack a standard.

Understanding the Structure

The structure of the CCSS for English Language Arts consists of three main sections:

- ✏ K–5 English Language Arts (Cross-disciplinary embedded into standards)
- ✏ 6–12 English Language Arts
- ✏ 6–12 Literacy in History/Social Studies, Science, and Technical Subjects

Each section is divided into strands:

- ✐ K–5 English Language Arts (Cross-disciplinary embedded into standards)
  - Reading
  - Writing
  - Speaking and Listening
  - Language

- ✐ 6–12 English Language Arts
  - Reading
  - Writing
  - Speaking and Listening
  - Language

- ✐ 6–12 Literacy in History/Social Studies, Science, and Technical Subjects
  - Reading
  - Writing

The Reading strand has three components:

- Reading: Literature (RL)
- Reading: Informational Text (RI)
- Reading: Foundational Skills

"The foundational skills apply only to grades K–5. These foundational skills are necessary and important components of an effective, comprehensive reading program designed to develop proficient readers with the capacity to comprehend texts across a range of types and disciplines" (http://www.corestandards.org/ELA-Literacy/RF/introduction).

Each strand has anchor standards. Both the reading and writing strands have 10 anchors each, and the speaking and listening and language standards have 6 anchors each to make a total of 32 anchor standards.

- Reading (10 anchors) ⚓ ⚓ ⚓ ⚓ ⚓ ⚓ ⚓ ⚓ ⚓ ⚓

- Writing (10 anchors) ⚓ ⚓ ⚓ ⚓ ⚓ ⚓ ⚓ ⚓ ⚓ ⚓

- Speaking and Listening (6 anchors) ⚓ ⚓ ⚓ ⚓ ⚓ ⚓

- Language (6 anchors) ⚓ ⚓ ⚓ ⚓ ⚓ ⚓

Figure 2.2 Common Core Strands and Clusters

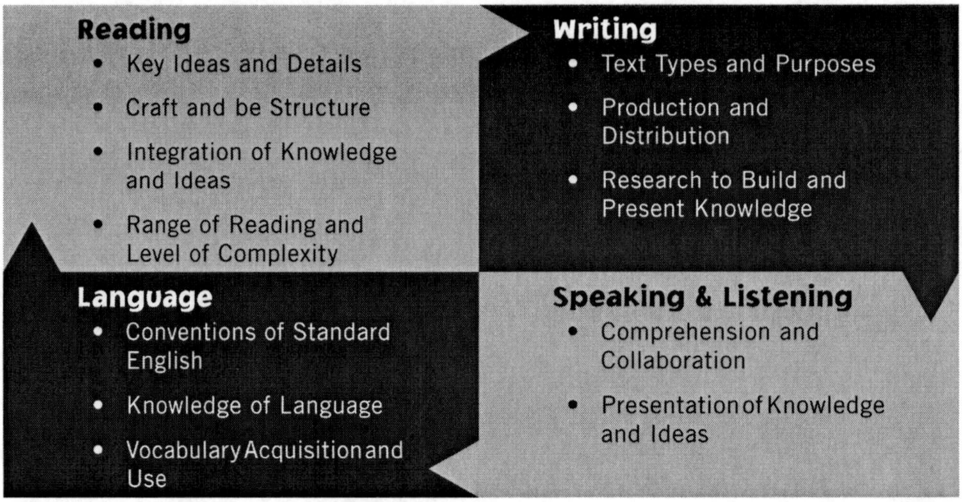

Reading
- Key Ideas and Details
- Craft and be Structure
- Integration of Knowledge and Ideas
- Range of Reading and Level of Complexity

Writing
- Text Types and Purposes
- Production and Distribution
- Research to Build and Present Knowledge

Language
- Conventions of Standard English
- Knowledge of Language
- Vocabulary Acquisition and Use

Speaking & Listening
- Comprehension and Collaboration
- Presentation of Knowledge and Ideas

Standards within the strands can easily overlap within lessons, thereby enabling the teacher to integrate multiple standards into literacy activities across the curriculum. The Common Core focuses on text to connect the literacy standards to each other. Reading, writing, speaking, listening, and language are interrelated and "intertwined in the structure of the standards, supporting and advancing effective practice through this blend" (O'Connor-Stockton 2013, slide 21).

> *Reading, writing, speaking, listening, and language are interrelated and "intertwined in the structure of the standards, supporting and advancing effective practice through this blend" (O'Connor-Stockton 2013).*

The CCSS also provide three appendices with additional information to further support teachers.

- ✏ Appendix A provides the research behind the standards. It explores the dimensions of text complexity and considers the various measurements. Supplements and support for the reading foundational skills for grades K–5 include charts and explanations for phoneme-grapheme correspondences, phonological awareness, and orthography as well as the definitions of the standards' three text types of writing. Also included in Appendix A is research that further supports the standards for Speaking and Listening and Language, along with a glossary of terms related to the standards.

- ✏ Appendix B presents reading text exemplars and corresponding performance tasks for all grade levels. Teachers are not required by the CCSS to use these particular texts, but the text lists and excerpts are strong models of grade-level complex text. The performance tasks typify the level of rigor and thinking required for students to respond to text(s) after reading.

- ✏ Appendix C supplies annotated student writing samples to allow teachers to view exemplars of students' writing at different grade levels. The student exemplars include argument, narrative, and informative/explanatory text types. The annotation for each student-written text details how the student met the writing standards within his or her composition.

Learning Progressions

> *A learning progression is a carefully sequenced set of building blocks that students must master en route to mastering a more distant curricular aim. These building blocks consist of subskills and bodies of enabling knowledge.*
> —Popham 2007

For each anchor standard, there are grade-level specific standards. These standards complement the broader anchor standards and are meant to be the benchmark for what students should be able to do and understand by the end of the school year. In effect, these standards follow a learning progression from kindergarten to 12th grade. This vertical alignment of standards ensures that student learning builds seamlessly from year to year so that when students graduate, they are college and career ready.

For example, Anchor Standard 1 for Reading states:

Read closely to determine what the text says explicitly and to make logical inferences from it; cite specific textual evidence when writing or speaking to support conclusions drawn from the text.

This is a broad anchor standard of what students need to understand and be able to do across kindergarten through 12th grade. However, each anchor standard is broken down into specific and age-appropriate supporting standards defined for each grade level that describe in detail what is expected for students at that level.

Note this Reading Literature Standard 1 specified for kindergarten:

With prompting and support, ask and answer questions about key details in a text.

This same standard for fifth grade is framed in this way:

Quote accurately from a text when explaining what the text says explicitly and when drawing inferences from the text.

By 11th and 12th grades, this same reading standard evolves into its full complexity:

Cite strong and thorough textual evidence to support analysis of what the text says explicitly as well as inferences drawn from the text, including determining where the text leaves matters uncertain.

You can see with this brief example how the challenge level of this particular standard increases significantly as our students progress through the grade levels. However, each grade-specific standard fits under the umbrella of the broader kindergarten through grade 12 anchor standards.

The following Common Core State Standards are from the Reading: Informational Text Standards. Anchor Standard 2 under the informational text standards focuses on determining central ideas or themes of a text and analyzing the development. The standards shown below represent how this standard looks at grades K, 1, 2, 3, 4, 5, 6, 7, 8, 9–10, and 11–12; however, they are not in sequence. See if you can organize these standards by complexity in order beginning with kindergarten and ending with grades 11–12. (An answer key is found at the end of this chapter.)

. . . .

_____ Determine a central idea of a text and analyze its development over the course of the text, including its relationship to supporting ideas; provide an objective summary of the text.

_____ Determine two or more main ideas of a text and explain how they are supported by key details; summarize the text.

_____ Identify the main topic of a multiparagraph text as well as the focus of specific paragraphs within the text.

_____ Determine two or more central ideas of a text and analyze their development over the course of the text, including how they interact and build on one another to provide a complex analysis; provide an objective summary of the text.

_____ Determine the main idea of a text and explain how it is supported by key details; summarize the text.

_____ Determine a central idea of a text and how it is conveyed through particular details; provide a summary of the text distinct from personal opinions or judgments.

_____ With prompting and support, identify the main topic and retell key details of a text.

_____ Determine two or more central ideas in a text and analyze their development over the course of the text; provide an objective summary of the text.

_____ Determine the main idea of a text; recount the key details and explain how they support the main idea.

_____ Determine a central idea of a text and analyze its development over the course of the text, including how it emerges and is shaped and refined by specific details; provide an objective summary of the text.

_____ Identify the main topic and retell key details of a text.

The Big Shifts

The authors of the ELA standards have taken careful measure to include some big, research-based literacy shifts. Students are expected to build knowledge through content-rich nonfiction and informational text as well as literary texts. All reading, writing, and speaking is grounded in evidence from text. And finally, students have regular practice with complex text and the accompanying shared, academic vocabulary. The six critical shifts are:

1. Balance informational and literary text.

2. Build knowledge in the disciplines.

3. Select text that reflects a "staircase of complexity."

4. Provide text-based answers.

5. Write from sources.

6. Increase academic vocabulary.

Shift 1: *more informational texts*

In reading, a shift in classrooms from reading mostly literary text with little nonfiction text to a purposeful balance of literature and informational texts reflects college and career ready expectations. With this increased "diet" of informational texts, students access a world of social studies, science, mathematics, the arts, and technology through wide reading across multiple genres of text. Since most of what adults read is informational text, many experts recommend that at least 50 percent of what students read in elementary school should be nonfiction text, with that percentage increasing through middle and high school (Coleman and Pimental 2012). Within the CCSS, teachers design instruction to teach students how to navigate, read, comprehend, and respond to nonfiction text through discussion, writing, and research. With increased exposure to informational text, students seem to self-select this text with greater frequency in their independent reading. In our years as teachers, we have never known an elementary student who didn't have a great passion for at least one nonfiction topic that could jettison that student into the exciting world of informational text. With a multitude of expertly written nonfiction text with rich vocabulary, intriguing text structures, and a plethora of colorful text features, students of all ages can find text that pulls them into the world of nonfiction.

Shift 2:

For K–5 classrooms, the CCSS embed content-area literacy into the standards, recognizing that under most circumstances, one teacher will instruct students across the day in literacy learning and content-area subjects. Therefore, the elementary standards do not include a separate section of literacy standards for content-area instruction as are found in the grades 6-12 standards entitled, "Literacy in History/Social Studies, Science, and Technical Subjects." These standards reflect the second shift: build knowledge in the disciplines. The grades 6–12 content-area standards emphasize the critical need for teachers outside the English/Language Arts (ELA) classroom to emphasize reading and writing experiences in their planning and instruction to build knowledge in the disciplines. Students are expected to learn from what they read and respond to that learning in multiple ways, including writing. These standards truly call for all teachers to be reading and writing teachers as these strategies and skills are essential for students in all contexts both throughout the school day and into their daily lives.

Shift 3:

Shift 3 requires that all students delve into grade-level complex text. As students move through school, text becomes incrementally both quantitatively and qualitatively complex. The CCSS refer to moving students up the "staircase of complexity" in text, progressing through ever-increasing increments of challenge as students proceed through the various grades in school. Appendix B in the CCSS gives multiple samples of this staircase of complexity by providing teachers with grade-band exemplar texts (literary and informational) that illustrate the text levels and types of text found at each "step" of the "staircase." Teachers carefully scaffold students into these often demanding texts by providing instructional time for careful, close reading of texts. These experiences ensure that students reading below grade level can have successful experiences in reading, comprehending, and responding to on-level text. Repeated readings as well as purposeful, text-dependent, high-level questions support students as they unearth the structures and deeper meanings within text. Teachers combine targeted modeling through thinking aloud about how to delve into text to dig out the layers of meaning with classroom discussions; daily focused, small-group instruction with specific feedback; powerful expert, intervention group time, using text just right for the students; and multiple opportunities to independently read text where they can read with at least 98 percent accuracy and 90 percent comprehension (Allington 2013). With this support, below-level students should be able to accelerate their learning and move into reading and processing increasingly challenging text, eventually reading grade-level complex text at an independent level.

Shift 4:

Shift 4 focuses on text-dependent answers to questions about text and text-dependent support for developing opinions/arguments about text whether in discussions about reading or writing a response to text. This shift requires that students carefully scrutinize the text to locate specific references to support their inferences about the text or in response to questions about the text. Students draw evidence or "proof" from the text to justify their thinking. We have found that kindergarteners can do this even at the earliest levels of reading text. When reading a book about a child going to the grocery store with her dad to buy different fruits and vegetables, these young students can easily return to the text to point out literal "proof" of what the child and dad put into their shopping cart, using both pictures and words in the text. These same students can find text evidence during an interactive read-aloud of a story to support inferential responses to questions such as, *What word would you pick to tell how Toad was feeling in* A Lost Button (Lobel 2003)? *Why did you pick that word? What is your evidence from the story?*

As students mature as readers and responders to literary and informational text, they continue to gather evidence and draw conclusions from increasingly complex text. The emphasis is on staying within the "four corners" of what the text actually states to provide evidence for reasonable inferences and not drawing on personal connections outside that text (Calkins 2012). Students use text information to understand the content and issues raised. The CCSS Speaking and Listening standards with a focus on formal and informal "talk" envision an environment where students have ample opportunities and time to co-construct meaning from text and defend their points of view and arguments through rich conversations grounded in text evidence.

Shift 5:

The CCSS call for a shared responsibility throughout the disciplines to support the writing standards. Argumentative writing is emphasized where students are expected to write sound arguments (opinions in grades kindergarten through five) on significant topics and issues backed by clear evidence from the text. When writing from sources, students are required not only to use multiple sources but also to evaluate those sources and the authors' perspectives and claims. In addition, in the upper grade levels, students examine counterclaims from different authors as part of their written analysis of sources. Writing from sources also includes reflecting on and analyzing literary texts from short stories to poetry to literature. Whether responding to literary or informational sources, students draw from text evidence to support their analysis and conclusions, and they synthesize ideas to write effective text in their own words, eventually using clear citations and sophisticated structure in their compositions.

Shift 6:

The Language standards on Vocabulary Acquisition and Use (Anchor Standards 4–6) and Anchor Standard 4 in Reading: Literature and Reading: Informational Text stress developing and understanding both general academic and domain-specific vocabulary and interpreting the language used in texts. Building a powerful repertoire of academic vocabulary is critical to reading and unearthing meaning in grade-level complex texts, reflecting and writing in response to reading, and negotiating meaning through thoughtful conversations about text. The CCSS suggest that language work should be intertwined throughout ELA and the content areas by weaving it into reading, writing, speaking, and listening in the classroom. Rather than rote memorization of vocabulary words, the focus of vocabulary instruction is on students selecting from a variety of flexible strategies to independently figure out the meaning of words and phrases (CCSS Language, Standard 4). These strategies include such actions as utilizing context clues, searching for meaningful word parts (such as affixes and roots), and clarifying meaning, when necessary, with vocabulary resources such as dictionaries and glossaries. Students are also required to demonstrate understanding of word nuances, word relationships, and figurative language. Through multiple opportunities to encounter and use new words in a variety of oral and written contexts and a targeted focus on vocabulary strategies and text comprehension, teachers consistently build students' ability to access increasingly complex text.

It is significant to note that these shifts reflected in the CCSS address reading, writing, and literacy across the curriculum and are included in literacy standards for science, social studies, and technical subjects. In actuality, these literacy standards represent a shift in thinking for instructional planning in the content areas, complementing rather than replacing content standards in those subjects. These anchor standards become the critical consideration for teachers in those specific disciplines, making literacy a shared responsibility for all educators.

"Unpacking" Standards

To "unpack" a standard is to determine what the standard exactly states, what it means for student learning, and what it calls for us, as teachers, to teach. The easiest way to do this is to break down the standard into component parts. Consider the following standard for third grade:

CCSS.ELA-Literacy.RI.3.2:

Determine the main idea of a text; recount the key details and explain how they support the main idea.

First, find the things (nouns) in the standard that students need to know. They need to know the main idea, text, key details, and main idea.

Determine the (main idea) of a (text); recount the (key details) and explain how they support the (main idea.)

Second, find the actions (verbs) in the standard that students are expected to do. They are expected to determine, recount, explain, and support.

(Determine) the main idea of a text; (recount) the key details and (explain) how they (support) the main idea.

Next, identify the key academic vocabulary from these two lists. For this example, we could identify *main idea*, *text*, *support*, and *key details* as our academic vocabulary. This vocabulary usually includes the nouns of the standard.

Then, rewrite the standard in student-friendly terms: *Students will identify the main idea of a text and use key details to explain and support the main idea.*

Finally, make a list of the skills students need in order to accomplish this standard. For this example, students would need the following skills:

- ✏ draw conclusions to determine main idea
- ✏ identify and explain key details that support the main idea

The following figure shows how this information can be broken down.

Figure 2.3 Unpacking the Standards

Common Core State Standard	Unpacking the Common Core State Standard		
	Student Target (use student-friendly language)	**What students need to know** (nouns)	**What students are to be able to do** (verbs)
CCSS.ELA-Literacy. RI.3.2: Determine the main idea of a text; recount the key details and explain how they support the main idea.	Students will identify the main idea of a text and use key details to explain and support the main idea. **Skills Needed:** drawing conclusions to determine main idea identifying and explaining key details that support main idea	main idea text key details	determine recount explain support
Key Vocabulary main idea, text, key details, support			

(Gladis 2013, slides 59–60)

Now, you try it. Select a standard. Identify the nouns and verbs, and write these in the chart (Figure 2.4). Then, select the new key vocabulary for your students from those words. Next, write the standard in student-friendly language. Finally, target the skills that students will need in order to accomplish this standard.

Figure 2.4 Unpacking the Standards—You Try It

Common Core State Standard	Unpacking the Common Core State Standard		
	Student Target (use student-friendly language)	What students need to know (nouns)	What students are to be able to do (verbs)
Choose a standard and write it here.	Write in student-friendly terms.	Find nouns in standard.	Find verbs in standard.
	<u>**Skills Needed**</u>: Identify skills needed.		
Key Vocabulary Identify academic vocabulary from your nouns and verbs.			

To get to the heart of what the standards mean for teachers and students, one must understand the structure of the standards. The standards are organized in a systematic way for easy understanding with very few differences between the K–5 and 6–12 standard organization. Learning progressions across the grade levels for each anchor standard are established to ensure student growth and success as each year's standards act as building blocks for mastering the necessary knowledge, concepts, and processes that students need to move forward. By breaking down the language of each standard into its significant parts, educators can know with certainty the specific requirements of the standard. However, as stated in the CCSS, *the standards define what all students are expected to know and be able to do, not how teachers should teach* (CCSS, Introduction). It is up to us, the educators, to unwrap the *how* for our instruction: How do we construct a powerful curriculum and employ expert pedagogy to ensure that the expectations of these standards are fulfilled in our classrooms?

Let's Think and Discuss

1. Why do you think it would be important to examine both the standards and the learning progression before and after your particular grade level? In what ways will understanding the learning progressions impact the way you plan your lessons?

2. Describe a lesson that you would deliver to teach toward a particular standard, and explain how that lesson supports learning progression of the standards.

Answer Key

K - 5 = main ideas
6 - 12 = central

8   Determine a central idea of a text and analyze its development over the course of the text, including its relationship to supporting ideas; provide an objective summary of the text.

5   Determine two or more main ideas of a text and explain how they are supported by key details; summarize the text.

2   Identify the main topic of a multi-paragraph text as well as the focus of specific paragraphs within the text.

11–12   Determine two or more central ideas of a text and analyze their development over the course of the text, including how they interact and build on one another to provide a complex analysis; provide an objective summary of the text.

4   Determine the main idea of a text and explain how it is supported by key details; summarize the text.

6   Determine a central idea of a text and how it is conveyed through particular details; provide a summary of the text distinct from personal opinions or judgments.

K   With prompting and support, identify the main topic and retell key details of a text.

7   Determine two or more central ideas in a text and analyze their development over the course of the text; provide an objective summary of the text.

3   Determine the main idea of a text; recount the key details and explain how they support the main idea.

9–10   Determine a central idea of a text and analyze its development over the course of the text, including how it emerges and is shaped and refined by specific details; provide an objective summary of the text.

1   Identify the main topic and retell key details of a text.

Chapter 3

Selecting Text That Works

> The text difficulty level is not the real issue. Instruction is. Teachers can scaffold and support students which will determine the amount of their learning and literacy independence.... The idea is not to either limit a student to a low-level text or allow him or her to struggle without support in a difficult text, but instead to provide texts and couple them with instruction.
> —Fisher, Frey, and Lapp 2012, 7–8

Suppose you were asked to rank the following books based on their text complexity. How would you rank these books from easiest (1) to most difficult (5)?

__4__ *To Kill a Mockingbird* by Harper Lee

__3__ *Harry Potter and the Deathly Hallows* by J.K. Rowling

__1__ *Bubble Trouble* by Margaret Mahy (Horn Book Winner)

__2__ *The Third Wheel (Diary of a Wimpy Kid, Book 7)* by Jeff Kinney

__5__ *The Grapes of Wrath* by John Steinbeck

Did you consider word length or familiarity? Were you thinking of word frequency, or the number of times a word appears in text? Perhaps you looked for simple, compound, complex, and compound complex sentences and ranked these texts accordingly. Maybe you considered text cohesion where a high level of text cohesion makes it easier for a reader to read and a low cohesion forces the reader to make many of the connections needed to comprehend the text.

Quite often, these factors are used to determine the instructional level of text. If your answers are "yes" to any of these factors, you were using *quantitative* measures to position text by difficulty. *Quantitative* is derived from the word *quantity*, having to do with numbers, and in this case, the readability and levels of these books can actually be evaluated using numerical formulas.

Qualitative	**Quantitative**	Reader and Task

There are multiple "readability" formulas used by various companies to "level" text. In these cases, the task of measuring and evaluating quantitative features of text is most often accomplished using computer software. The CCSS refer to Lexile® levels of quantitative text features (developed by MetaMetrics) to exemplify a range of text complexity. These Lexile® ranges have been, in turn, realigned to meet the rigor of the CCSS grade level text complexity bands.

Figure 3.1 Text Complexity and Lexile® Ranges

Text Complexity Grade Band in the CCSS	Lexile® Ranges Aligned to CCSS Expectations
K–1	N/A
2–3	420–820
4–5	740–1010
6–8	925–1185
9–10	1050–1335
11–CCR	1185–1385

Quantitative measures are used to assign a readability level to a text based on factors such as syntax and sentence length, text cohesion, word length, word frequency, and word familiarity.

> Syntax and sentence length place varying processing demands on the reader encountering multiple sentence structures, sentence length (words per sentence), and features such as dependent/independent clauses, prepositional phrases, pronouns, adverbs, and adjectives, etc.

✏ Text cohesion (addressed in the Coh-Metrix system of measuring readability) attempts to examine the ways text is held together semantically to support or challenge the reader (see CCSS, Appendix A). Factors such as concrete language, repetition, and transitions serve to connect the text for the reader by establishing meaningful relationships between words, sentences, paragraphs, and ideas. A highly cohesive text would support a reader and be easier to read. A text with lower cohesion would greatly challenge a reader. Several important points to consider include the following:

1. The analysis of syntax and sentence length is based on the overall text. Therefore, the text could vary in difficulty between pages or even paragraphs.

2. A shorter sentence could be difficult for a reader to comprehend based on the concept presented, vocabulary, or inference necessary to comprehend the author's message.

3. Text cohesion is not yet calibrated to the CCSS text complexity bands, but it does provide a variety of new factors to consider in quantitative analysis of text (see CCSS, Appendix A).

✏ At the word level, readability formulas for text complexity consider the word challenge level of text. How long are the words? How many syllables do they have? How often do the words occur in the text? How familiar are the words to a reader of that text? How frequently do these words generally appear in print? Nonfiction text is often assigned a higher quantitative level because of the frequent occurrence of content-specific vocabulary. These words are counted each time they appear in a text to determine the overall text level. While longer words or less-frequently encountered words, especially specific content-area words, do increase the quantitative complexity of a text, we have often encountered first grade students who can easily read long words such as *transportation* or *hippopotamus* once they have had an initial introduction to the word and its meaning. Therefore, this new word would not continue to be a challenge for the students when it appears multiple times in a text. Similarly, we have seen students identified as "below-grade-level readers" who successfully read a grade-level nonfiction text on a personal high-interest topic. This happens when the majority of the content-area words and concepts are familiar to the reader. For example, Evan, a sixth grade student reading independently at the second–third grade text complexity band was a shark fanatic, and the quantitative features of a higher Lexile® level shark book did not keep him from enthusiastically tackling the challenge and reading the text.

Returning to our original consideration of the five texts you ranked at the beginning of this chapter, if you used only *quantitative* measures to describe the complexity of these books, based on Lexile® levels, the books from our example are ranked like this:

1. *The Grapes of Wrath*—680, grade level band 2nd–3rd

2. *To Kill a Mockingbird*—870, grade level band 4th–5th

3. *Harry Potter and the Deathly Hallows*—980, grade level band 5th–8th

4. *The Third Wheel (Diary of a Wimpy Kid)*—1060, grade level band 6th–9th

5. *Bubble Trouble*—1240, grade level band 9th–12th

Does this ranking shock you? Many teachers are surprised to find that *Diary of Wimpy Kid* falls at such a high grade level band because they have witnessed first graders who can't get enough of this book. This information raises many questions: Is it appropriate to give second grade students *The Grapes of Wrath* to read? Does it mean that students in 10th grade would be reading a picture book called *Bubble Trouble*? Although "readable," it is unlikely that *Grapes of Wrath* would be an appropriate text for a second grade student any more than *Bubble Trouble* would be a high-interest text for a 10th grader. But, the rich language of this picture book makes it a wonderful adult-directed read-aloud for pre-kindergarten children through second graders. It is important to keep in mind that "ultimately it is the reader who decides the difficulty of a text" (Fisher, Frey, Lapp 2012, 22) as he or she attempts to read that text. While understanding the quantitative level of texts is important, it is not the *only* factor teachers should consider when determining complexity of texts.

Return to our ranking of the five texts. Maybe you thought about quantitative features as you ordered the texts by perceived difficulty or challenge, but perhaps you considered other factors as well while you leveled these texts. Did you think about the explicit or implicit levels of meaning in the text? Perhaps you considered the structure of the text as either being conventional and straightforward or unconventionally organized with flashbacks, flash forwards, or cause and effect relationships. Could it be that you thought about the language clarity, content-specific words, and the literal versus figurative vocabulary used in the texts? Maybe you looked at the knowledge demands—the background needed to successfully negotiate the meaning of the text.

If your answers are "yes" to any of these factors, you were using *qualitative* measures to order these texts. *Qualitative* is derived from the word *quality*, having to do with the particular attributes, features and characteristics, and level of meaning within these books.

| Qualitative | Quantitative | Reader and Task |

In thinking about text structure, these are the questions you might have asked:

➫ How complex is the structure of the text?

➫ Is the story told in chronological order, or are there flashbacks and other manipulations of time?

➫ Is any informational text laid out in a clear format of a main idea with details and simple graphics to help convey meaning, or are other nonfiction text structures present with more sophisticated graphics that may provide information outside the actual text?

Considering the language conventionality and clarity, you could have asked:

➫ Does the text contain language that is familiar, clear, and straightforward?

➫ Is the text "conversational" with lots of dialogue, or is it more academic and content-oriented?

➫ Does the text contain an abundance of academic vocabulary, words with multiple meanings, or figurative and/or unfamiliar language?

Looking at the levels of meaning and knowledge demands of text, you may have thought:

- What are the themes or main ideas of this text? Are there multiple layers of meaning and complexity?

- Is the purpose of the text explicitly given, or does the reader have to infer it from reading?

- How much background knowledge would a student need in order to understand this selection?

- Does the text, if discipline-specific, support the reader by building knowledge and understanding within the text?

(See the chart in the CCSS Appendix A, page 6, for further elaboration on qualitative measures of text.)

If you considered these qualitative features of text, the list of text that you made might have looked more like this:

1. *Bubble Trouble*—1240, grade level band 9th–12th

2. *The Third Wheel (Diary of a Wimpy Kid*, Book 7*)*—1060, grade level band 6th–9th

3. *Harry Potter and the Deathly Hallows*—980, grade level band 5th–8th

4. *To Kill a Mockingbird*—870, grade level band 4th–5th

5. *The Grapes of Wrath*—680, grade level band 2nd–3rd

Return to our ranking of the five texts one last time. Perhaps you considered factors other than just quantitative and qualitative as you leveled these texts. Did you base your rating on what your students would be motivated to read? Maybe you determined the list according to your students' personal backgrounds and experiences. You might have wondered about their purpose for reading the texts.

If your answers are "yes" to any of these factors, you were considering *reader and task measures.*

Reflecting on both the reader and the task of reading and responding to a selected text is the final segment of the text complexity triangle. For this factor, the teacher's personal knowledge of students gained through assessments, observations, and informal discussions becomes a strong basis for selecting instructional text for students or supporting them as they select their own text for independent reading. When students choose their own texts based on their interests or the instructional task at hand, they become invested in the reading process. In turn, students experience a sense of self-efficacy as they encounter reading challenges and endeavor to problem-solve tricky parts "on the run" using known, effective strategies in order to continue reading.

We begin to broaden our thinking and consider the context that surrounds the text, pondering questions such as:

- Are the students motivated to read the text?

- Are they interested in the topic?

- What is their knowledge of the subject prior to beginning to read?

- What response or task are they being asked to do after reading the text?

Reader and task considerations are powerful factors impacting student reading success and do not always align with quantitative or qualitative measures of the level where we "think" a student might be reading. When students have read previous, easier books in a series such as *The Diary of a Wimpy Kid* or *Harry Potter*, or have seen a movie based on the book, they often want to read another book about those characters because their schema is established. If a text is popular among students—"everybody" is reading it— then students might want to read the book no matter how simple or challenging the text is for that reader. We often smile thinking about the kindergartener some years back seen "reading" *Harry Potter and the Sorcerer's Stone*. As the child "read," he or she carefully turned a page at a time, scanning the text from top to bottom. The child seemed oblivious to the fact that the book was upside down! On the other hand, Jordan, a precocious, strong reader successfully tackled *The Lightning Thief* by Rick Riordan as a first-grader. Many students enjoy informational texts written by favorite authors on elevated text levels because of the familiarity of the topic or strong text features like illustrations, photographs, and cut-away diagrams that support meaning as seen in books from the *DK Eyewitness Books* series. Other students like historical fiction, especially when their text choices are linked with current social studies content. There is little doubt that this third measure of text complexity directly affects students' reading interest and stamina!

If you thought about reader and task considerations, your list might have looked more like this:

1. *The Third Wheel (Diary of a Wimpy Kid, Book 7)*—1060, grade level band 6th–9th

2. *Harry Potter and the Deathly Hallows*—980, grade level band 5th–8th

3. *Bubble Trouble*—1240, grade level band 9th–12th

4. *To Kill a Mockingbird*—870, grade level band 4th–5th

5. *The Grapes of Wrath*—680, grade level band 2nd–3rd

According to the CCSS Appendix A, *The standards presume that all **three elements** will come into play when text complexity and appropriateness are determined* (5). This means that teachers must simultaneously address the quantitative, qualitative, and reader and task factors when selecting texts for close readings, anchor lessons, and instructional groups, or when supporting students in finding "just right" texts for independent reading.

How to Determine Text Complexity

Now that you understand the three levels of text complexity, let's focus on how to determine complex texts appropriate for your students. While there are many ways to determine text complexity, we would like to propose a set of four easy steps:

1. Consider the quantitative measures of the text.

2. Analyze the qualitative measures of the text.

3. Reflect upon the reader and task considerations.

4. Recommend the placement in the appropriate text complexity band.

Figure 3.2 Evaluation of Text Complexity

Those Who Overcame

Not long ago in the United States, African Americans had to live by different rules than other people. They were **segregated**. This means that they were separated from white people. They could not share restrooms, drinking fountains, or parks. They had to sit in the backs of buses and movie theaters.

The Civil Rights Movement of the 1950s and 1960s, led by Dr. Martin Luther King Jr., helped put an end to segregation. But many people held onto their **prejudices** (PREJ-uh-dis-iz) against African Americans. A prejudice is an unfair opinion formed without facts or evidence. Prejudices put African Americans at a disadvantage.

Figure 3.2 is an excerpt from a book titled *African Americans Today* by Stephanie Kuligowski from a Primary Source Readers collection. Please note that in evaluating a text for complexity, the teacher would consider the entire text to be read by the students. For this example only, we have included just a short portion of this text.

Step 1

Determining text complexity asks us to look at the quantitative level of the book. Remember, the quantitative measure is only one of the three parts of the text complexity triangle.

Qualitative	Quantitative	Reader and Task

For this example, we can use Lexile® levels to determine quantitative instructional level. Read the text again. What do you think the recommended Lexile® level might be?

If we look only at quantitative measures, we find that the publishers of this book have included the Lexile® level on the back book cover—the 820 Lexile® range. This text falls within the second to third grade text complexity band, but does that necessarily mean that it is appropriate reading material for second and third grade students? The answer is an obvious *no*! Reflect back to the Lexile® Framework for Reading for the *The Grapes of Wrath*. This Pulitzer-Prize winning book is at this same readability level because it expresses complex ideas in familiar words and simple syntax, much of it in the form of dialogue (O'Connor-Stockton 2013, slide 89). According to the standards, *The Grapes of Wrath is* a ninth or tenth grade-level appropriate text. Therefore, it makes sense to us that we should not make a decision on how and with whom to use this book in our classroom instructional context before considering Steps 2 and 3. Our final recommendation may be validated, influenced, or even overruled by our examination of qualitative measures and reader and task considerations (O'Connor-Stockton 2013, slide 90).

Step 2

This process asks us to look at the qualitative level of the book. Remember, the qualitative measure is the second of the three parts of the text complexity triangle.

Figure 3.3 can help teachers measure the qualitative aspects of the text.

Figure 3.3 Qualitative Measures Rubric

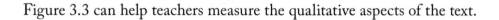

Text Complexity: Qualitative Measures Rubric

INFORMATIONAL TEXTS

Text Title _____   Text Author _____

	Exceedingly Complex	Very Complex	Moderately Complex	Slightly Complex
TEXT STRUCTURE	○ **Organization:** Connections between an extensive range of ideas, processes or events are deep, intricate and often ambiguous; organization is intricate or discipline-specific ○ **Text Features:** If used, are essential in understanding content ○ **Use of Graphics:** If used, intricate, extensive graphics, tables, charts, etc., are extensive and integral to making meaning of the text; may provide information not otherwise conveyed in the text	○ **Organization:** Connections between an expanded range ideas, processes or events are often implicit or subtle; organization may contain multiple pathways or exhibit some discipline-specific traits ○ **Text Features:** If used, directly enhance the reader's understanding of content ○ **Use of Graphics:** If used, graphics, tables, charts, etc. support or are integral to understanding the text	○ **Organization:** Connections between some ideas or events are implicit or subtle; organization is evident and generally sequential or chronological ○ **Text Features:** If used, enhance the reader's understanding of content ○ **Use of Graphics:** If used, graphic, pictures, tables, and charts, etc. are mostly supplementary to understanding the text	○ **Organization:** Connections between ideas, processes or events are explicit and clear; organization of text is chronological, sequential or easy to predict ○ **Text Features:** If used, help the reader navigate and understand content but are not essential to understanding content. ○ **Use of Graphics:** If used, graphic, pictures, tables, and charts, etc. are simple and unnecessary to understanding the text but they may support and assist readers in understanding the written text
LANGUAGE FEATURES	○ **Conventionality:** Dense and complex; contains considerable abstract, ironic, and/or figurative language ○ **Vocabulary:** Complex, generally unfamiliar, archaic, subject-specific, or overly academic language; may be ambiguous or purposefully misleading ○ **Sentence Structure:** Mainly complex sentences with several subordinate clauses or phrases and transition words; sentences often contains multiple concepts	○ **Conventionality:** Fairly complex; contains some abstract, ironic, and/or figurative language ○ **Vocabulary:** Fairly complex language that is sometimes unfamiliar, archaic, subject-specific, or overly academic ○ **Sentence Structure:** Many complex sentences with several subordinate phrases or clauses and transition words	○ **Conventionality:** Largely explicit and easy to understand with some occasions for more complex meaning ○ **Vocabulary:** Mostly contemporary, familiar, conversational; rarely overly academic ○ **Sentence Structure:** Primarily simple and compound sentences, with some complex constructions	○ **Conventionality:** Explicit, literal, straightforward, easy to understand ○ **Vocabulary:** Contemporary, familiar, conversational language ○ **Sentence Structure:** Mainly simple sentences
PURPOSE	○ **Purpose:** Subtle and intricate, difficult to determine; includes many theoretical or abstract elements	○ **Purpose:** Implicit or subtle but fairly easy to infer; more theoretical or abstract than concrete	○ **Purpose:** Implied but easy to identify based upon context or source	○ **Purpose:** Explicitly stated, clear, concrete, narrowly focused
KNOWLEDGE DEMANDS	○ **Subject Matter Knowledge:** Relies on extensive levels of discipline-specific or theoretical knowledge; includes a range of challenging abstract concepts ○ **Intertextuality:** Many references or allusions to other texts or outside ideas, theories, etc.	○ **Subject Matter Knowledge:** Relies on moderate levels of discipline-specific or theoretical knowledge; includes a mix of recognizable ideas and challenging abstract concepts ○ **Intertextuality:** Some references or allusions to other texts or outside ideas, theories, etc.	○ **Subject Matter Knowledge:** Relies on common practical knowledge and some discipline-specific content knowledge; includes a mix of simple and more complicated, abstract ideas ○ **Intertextuality:** Few references or allusions to other texts or outside ideas, theories etc	○ **Subject Matter Knowledge:** Relies on everyday, practical knowledge; includes simple, concrete ideas ○ **Intertextuality:** No references or allusions to other texts or outside ideas, theories, etc.

(http://www.achievethecore.org/content/upload/SCASS_Info_Text_Complexity_Qualitative_Measures_Info_Rubric_2.8.pdf)

This rubric contains four keys: text structure, language features, purpose, and knowledge demands. The ratings are as follows: Exceedingly Complex, Very Complex, Moderately Complex, and Slightly Complex. In this example, we just consider the knowledge demands for our identified text selection.

Looking through the entire book *African Americans Today*, a teacher finds that the topics include segregation, the Civil Rights Movement, the Los Angeles riots in response to the Rodney King verdict, and affirmative action. The descriptors within the rubrics help a teacher make these qualitative knowledge demand determinations. We feel that this book selection would be rated as Middle High as shown in the example below.

> **Middle High**:
>
> **Subject Matter Knowledge**: requires moderate levels of discipline-specific content knowledge; some theoretical knowledge may enhance understanding.
>
> **Intertextuality**: some references to/citations of other texts or outside ideas, theories, etc.

The teacher then considers the other factors of qualitative text complexity from the chart to get a sense of what students would need to know to be set up to effectively read and understand this book.

Step 3

This process asks us to examine any reader and task considerations for our own particular students, which is the final leg of the three parts of the text complexity triangle.

| Qualitative | Quantitative | **Reader and Task** |

Teachers need to reflect on their students' strengths and interests as well as any task students might be expected to perform in response to the text. How would these factors impact your evaluation of the text complexity for your students and this text?

Step 4

In Step 4, the teacher recommends placement in the appropriate text complexity band. All of the preceding factors work together to help teachers make decisions about text complexity and where the canon of text falls within the bands, the range of readability, your task expectations, and the individual students you face each day.

The CCSS Appendix A says *such assessments are best made by the classroom teachers employing their professional judgment, experience, and knowledge of their students and the subject* (4). In other words, the teacher makes the recommendation.

How Do You Do It?

So, how does reflection on the quantitative dimensions, qualitative features, and reader and task considerations support us as we make instructional decisions for our students? The stakes are stacked high. The CCSS expect students to *comprehend and evaluate complex texts across a range of types and disciplines . . . [and] adapt their communication in relation to audience, task, purpose, and discipline* (7). In fact, Reading Anchor Standard 10 states that students will "Read and comprehend complex literary and informational texts independently and proficiently."

Each classroom teacher has to make his or her own decisions about how successfully students are performing within a text complexity band and with individual texts. To accomplish Reading Anchor Standard 10, teachers must ask themselves what kind of scaffolding is needed to challenge students at the very cusp of their current learning level *and* how to accelerate student reading below-grade-level into grade-level complex text.

It is important for teachers to watch out for "level-boundedness" or lack of authentic, challenging reading work. Students must move beyond accurate "word-calling" at any given level to real, deep comprehension of what they read. Teachers must monitor students for effective strategic processing of literary and informational text as students move up the complexity bands. Teachers strive to push the boundaries and recognize that students can sometimes handle harder quantitative text measures if we scaffold the qualitative dimensions, thereby, actually enabling students to handle more complex text. Below-level readers need daily supported opportunities to read and process grade-level complex text and respond as on-level thinkers, while higher-level readers need challenging opportunities to think deeply about text that is appropriate for them.

However, as Allington so succinctly states, *you can't learn much from books that you can't read* (2001). Students cannot comprehend text that they cannot decode. These students need daily "teacher time" in a small group context to read text at their current instructional level in order to help them develop effective reading strategies and accelerate their reading growth. Through teacher-guided instruction with targeted feedback, these students experience extended successful engagements with text. Below-level readers learn to problem-solve based on an ever-increasing repertoire of strategies, and eventually their instructional reading levels are accelerated to reach grade-level goals.

Therefore, the instructional context along with the level of scaffolding necessary to ensure that students successfully navigate and comprehend text impacts the selection of text. A significant instructional model linked to the CCSS is close reading where teachers scaffold students as necessary into deep thinking about text. For close reading experiences, the text chosen is grade-level, complex text representing a variety of genres in order to give students the opportunity to discover and process multiple layers of meaning (essential in the CCSS). At other times, when the teacher needs to demonstrate something that good readers do as they read and think about text (providing a metacognitive model of a strategic process), the text complexity of the featured text will still probably be at grade level since the teacher is doing the reading and "thinking aloud" about the text. The focus of the modeled "anchor" lesson—the instructional goal and behavior—drives the text selection as the teacher matches the text with the teaching focus.

Shared/interactive reading practice gives students an opportunity to "try on" what has just been modeled. Therefore, the students may all share-read a grade-level, complex text and work through the text in teacher-led collegial academic conversations. In another scenario, the students might partner or work in small groups on texts at their instructional level, incorporating shared practice of the teaching focus, while the teacher moves between groups to monitor and further engage students in practicing the teaching focus within their text. These instructional choices are driven by how the teacher wishes to orchestrate the interactive practice of shared, strategic negotiating of meaning from text.

When meeting with a small instructional group, the teacher pulls together students with similar learning goals. Many times, this group will read at approximately the same text level, and so teachers' knowledge of the features of text complexity and the students' learning strengths and needs enhances the lesson by ensuring that teachers select a "good fit" text for guided practice, employing the teaching objectives/goals. Teachers may also utilize strategy groups where students come together in a small group to solidify and practice a strategic process in their reading. In this setting, students may each bring a text from their self-selected reading that is on their *independent* reading level to use as they read small chunks of text, employ the strategy, and then discuss their thoughts with the teacher and their group.

Text complexity considerations also frame the independent reading context in the classroom. Whether you have classroom libraries or allow students to select their independent text from a school library or other sources, the key element here is that the text is indeed on the reader's independent text level. The savvy teacher recognizes that quantitative, qualitative, and reader/task considerations are all in play when students self-select texts for independent reading. Sometimes what students select for independent reading is not just about a "just right" quantitative text level, but also about students' interest and motivation to complete a particular text. Chapters 5–8 further address close reading, modeled lessons, shared/interactive reading, small guided instructional groups, and independent reading as critical instructional contexts for embedding the CCSS.

How to Create Text Sets

The CCSS directly address how students must comprehend and analyze multiple text types. They state, "*Students comprehend and evaluate complex texts across a range of types and disciplines… adapt their communication in relation to audience, task, purpose, and discipline*" (2010, 7).

College and Career Anchor Standards for Reading: *Students will analyze how two or more texts address similar themes or topics in order to build knowledge or to compare the approaches authors take* (R.9).

Since the standards demand explicit instruction in analyzing and comparing different kinds of texts, teachers must intentionally plan for intertextuality. According to Anstey and Bull, intertextuality refers to *the ways one text might draw on or resemble the characteristics of another, causing the reader of the texts to make links between them.* (2006, 30). Creating text sets is a perfect solution for organizing texts for this kind of integrated instruction. Text sets are rich collections of text and other resources that go beyond *just* books to include multi-modal print and digital resources. Text sets can include primary sources, blogs, images, tagged websites, interviews, newspaper articles, magazine articles, videos, and podcasts, to name a few.

Text sets are most often organized around a central theme, topic, or concept. They can be utilized in reading/English/Language Arts and/or the content areas. Teachers should strive to build text sets that are:

1. multileveled (representative of a span of text reading levels)

2. multimodal (includes digital resources in addition to more traditional texts)

3. multigenre (realistic fiction, fantasy, historical fiction, mystery, science fiction, traditional literature, poetry, nonfiction, etc.).

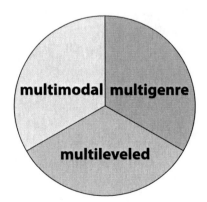

For example, a text set focused on the topic of tornadoes might include nonfiction books about tornadoes, fiction books centered on characters' encounters with a tornado, tornado poems, newspaper or magazine articles, captioned graphics, recorded weather reports, videos, and written personal accounts. This text set represents multiple genres and includes multimodal materials. Note that when we build text sets for students to use, we do not limit the range of text. While many of these tornado texts and resources will be on-grade-level text, the text set will also include easier texts and above-level texts, making the text set multileveled and, thereby, differentiated so all students can access the topic content and build knowledge. With any necessary guidance, all students can find text within the set that will both challenge and motivate them. We have found that less-experienced readers excitedly read photographs, charts, diagrams, and other nonfiction text features to gain information from a book or magazine that might be too difficult for them to actually decode the text's words. By its nature, the text set provides the text and resources necessary to allow students to select "just right" reading selections, comprehend what they read, respond to guiding questions, and develop essential understandings and meaning.

Reading within content-area driven text sets helps students reach a multifaceted, deep understanding of the featured content, topic, or theme, while, at the same time, providing students the opportunity to actively use reading, writing, listening, speaking, and language skills/standards so they can communicate what they have learned (Cappiello and Dawes 2013). In other words, by integrating literacy strategies and skills into engagements with well-constructed texts sets, students gain and communicate deep content-area knowledge. When teachers make the transition from textbook-only classrooms to multi-text classrooms, the focus of study becomes concepts rather than the content of one particular book. Students gain both a broad perspective and an in-depth sense of the subject matter from reading many texts on the same topic (Ivey 2002, 20). Text sets have many other benefits such as helping students confront multiple perspectives (Freedman 2011).

Depending on the purpose, students can use text sets in many settings such as independent reading, small instructional groups, literature or inquiry discussion groups, or content-area research. The tornado text set described previously could be part of a broader umbrella theme such as "Man vs. Nature" or "Forces of Nature" and be used during reading/language arts or science. By reading multiple selections in the text set, students participate in a classroom community of learners developing meaning and building knowledge from comparing, contrasting, analyzing, and evaluating a variety of texts.

Here are a few examples of text sets developed for elementary students. These text sets are "under construction," as the teacher (and students) can continue to add texts. Note how the text sets are multilevel, multimodal, and multigenre.

Theme: Perseverance (grades 2–4)

More Than Anything Else by Marie Bradby (1995)

Video introduction of the book, *More Than Anything Else*, http://www.youtube.com/watch?v=gsDW4E0jiKo

Booker T. Washington by Thomas Amper and Jeni Reeves (2001)

"Cast Down Your Bucket Where You Are": Booker T. Washington's Atlanta Compromise Speech (Gives young readers a chance just to hear Washington's voice) (1895)

Photographs of Booker T. Washington from Library of Congress

The Hard-Times Jar by Ethel Footman Smothers (2003)

The Other Side by Jacqueline Woodson (2001)

Momma, Where Are You From? by Mary Bradby and Chris Soentpiet (2000)

Thank You, Mr. Falker by Patricia Polacco (2012)

The Wednesday Surprise by Eve Bunting (1989)

Please Bury Me in the Library by J. Patrick Lewis (2005)

Wilma Unlimited by Kathleen Krull (2000)

Topic: Tornadoes (grades 2–5)

Investigating Storms by Debra J. Housel, TCM Science Reader: Earth and Space Science (2008)

Weather Scientists by Debra J. Housel, Robin S. Doak, and Bradford Kendall, TCM Science Reader: Earth and Space Science (2008)

Tornadoes and Hurricanes (TIME for Kids Nonfiction Readers) by Cy Armour (2011)

Tornadoes: Geology and Weather by William B. Rice, TCM Science Reader: A Closer Look (2009).

How a Tornado Forms diagram and informational card from *Exploring Writing, Level 3*

Tornadoes, from *Kids Discover* Magazine (1996)

Tornadoes by Seymour Simon (2001)

Night of the Twisters by Ivy Ruckman (2003)

Twisters on Tuesday (*Magic Tree House #23*) by Mary Pope Osborne (2001)

Magic Tree House Fact Tracker #8: Twisters and Other Terrible Storms: A Nonfiction Companion to Magic Tree House #23 by Will Osborne, Mary Pope Osborne, and Sal Murdocca (2003)

Twister: The Science of Tornadoes and the Making of an Adventure Movie by Keay Davidson (1996)

Natural Disasters (True Tales) by Madeline Boskey (2003)

Video clips showing tornadoes from the National Geographic website

Newspaper articles and firsthand accounts of tornadoes

Weather reports

Map of tornado alley

Text sets are also essential for secondary students. Consider the following possible text set:

Concept: Bullying (Secondary)

Priscilla and the Wimps by Richard Peck (from *Past Perfect and Present Tense: New and Collected Stories* (2004)

Holes by Louis Sachar (2000)

Middle School: How I Survived Bullies, Broccoli, and Snake Hill by James Patterson and Chris Tebbetts (2013)

The Juice Box Bully: Empowering Kids to Stand Up For Others by Bob Sornson, Maria Dismondy, and Kim Shaw (2010)

The Recess Queen by Alexis O'Neill and Laura Huliska-Beith (2002)

Stick Up for Yourself: Every Kid's Guide to Personal Power and Positive Self-Esteem by Gershen Kaufman, Lev Raphael, and Pamela Espeland (1999)

Current newspaper and magazine articles about bullying

Clips from *The Karate Kid* movie (1984, 2010)

Clips from *Back to the Future* movie (1985)

PBS website for students: http://pbskids.org/itsmylife/friends/bullies

"What Kids Say About Bullying" article retrieved from http://kidshealth.org/kid/feeling/school/poll_bullying.html

The following example is for secondary to help students develop the ability to discern perspectives. While World War II can be a huge topic of study, we want to narrow down the focus so that, while a history class could definitely use this, a language arts class could use it as well and enter history in a different way. Notice that the websites, movies, fiction books, primary sources, and nonfiction are all at different reading levels.

Concept/Topic: Faces of War—World War II (Secondary)

V-mail primary source letters from an American soldier to his family

Dear Miss Breed: True Stories of the Japanese American Incarceration During World War II and a Librarian Who Made a Difference by Joanne Oppenheim (2006)

Letters from Iwo Jima (2006) movie clips

Flags of Our Fathers (2006) movie clips

Horton Hears a Who and *Yertle the Turtle* by Dr. Seuss (Theodore S. Geisel appears to have buried both political and moral issues within these two Dr. Seuss books. *Yertle the Turtle* is a parable about Hitler's rise to power. *Horton Hears a Who*, written after Geisel visited post-World War II Japan, is a message for all people. The tiny Whos symbolize those defeated people who are not too "little" to be important to their country and their government. The lesson from this book is summed up in the famous line *a person is a person no matter how small.*

Baseball Saved Us by Ken Mochizuki (1993)

Code Talker: A Novel About The Navajo Marines of World War Two by Joseph Bruchac (2005)

The Orphans of Normandy: A True Story of World War II Told Through Drawings by Children by Nancy Amis (2003)

The Last Good War: The Faces and Voices of World War II by Thomas Sanders

The Faces of World War II by Max Hastings (2008)

Remember, Rome was not built in a day. Likewise, the best text sets are built over time. Begin by looking in your own classroom library for resources. Peruse your school and public libraries, local bookstores, online sources, and random garage sales to find texts and multimodal resources to add to your collections. Often, students have resources to contribute, so ask them to help you build these text sets for an upcoming unit of study. Subscribe to magazines and use the various articles in text sets. (The articles are also great for small group instruction)

The following form, Figure 3.4, can be used to help organize your resources, ensuring that the texts you select are multigenre, multileveled, and multimodal. Keeping this form for the various text sets you develop in a folder or notebook will provide you a permanent record of the texts you used when you are ready to set up the text set for another year. Be sure to list where you got the resource and where you are storing it for easy access later on. Remember, building great text sets is an ongoing process. This form is meant to be added to each year as you find more and more possible texts to include.

Figure 3.4 Selecting Texts

Topic, Concept, or Theme:				
Resource	**Where Can I Find It?**	**Multigenre** Fiction (what kind?) Nonfiction (what kind?)	**Multimodal** Digital Print Audio Video	**Multileveled** Approximate Text Level

Let's Think and Discuss

1. What are some ways that you can incorporate text sets with your students?

2. Think about one of your struggling readers. What can you apply from this chapter to help you scaffold your reading instruction so that this student can climb that "staircase of complexity"?

Chapter

Identifying Higher-Order Thinking Within the CCSS

> *Critical thinking is best understood as the ability of thinkers to take charge of their own thinking. This requires that they develop sound criteria and standards for analyzing and assessing their own thinking and routinely use those criteria and standards to improve its quality.*
>
> —Elder and Paul 1994, 34–35

A question many teachers may ask is: How do I get my students to use higher-order thinking skills? Older, inquisitive students value the challenge of these questions and beg their teachers, "Give me the opportunity to think deeper!" As teachers, we can sometimes feel burdened with the task of getting our students to engage in higher-order thinking. Sometimes, we wonder if we are doing it right or if the questions we pose are deep enough. Reflecting on the quote above, we note that higher-order thinking is characterized by reflective, evaluative, and analytical thinking.

While the CCSS does not specifically use the term "higher-order thinking," to meet many of the CCSS anchor standards, students must use higher-order thinking to achieve the expectations stated. The following examples are taken from the anchor standards in reading, writing, speaking and listening, and language. After each standard in italics, a brief elaboration points out how higher-order thinking is involved for that standard.

Anchor Standards for Reading

Key Ideas and Details

1. **Read closely to determine what the text says explicitly and to make logical inferences from it; cite specific textual evidence when writing or speaking to support conclusions drawn from that text.** When students make logical inferences from a text they have read, they are using higher-order thinking because the answers are not found directly in the text. Students must "read between the lines" of the text to make reasonable inferences based on text evidence.

2. **Determine central ideas or themes of a text and analyze their development; summarize the key supporting details and ideas.** When students decide on the themes/central ideas of a text and analyze the development of those themes/ideas, they are using higher-order thinking because they are looking at the intended purpose of the author in developing theme/ideas throughout the text.

3. **Analyze how and why individuals, events, or ideas develop and interact over the course of a text.** Analyzing the how and why, when the text is not explicit about the how and why, is higher-order thinking.

Craft and Structure

4. **Interpret words and phrases as they are used in a text, including determining technical, connotative, and figurative meanings, and analyze how specific word choices shape meaning or tone.** Simply telling the meaning of words is not necessarily higher-order thinking, but when students have to infer word meanings from context or make deep connections about the meanings behind figurative language and authors' word choices, then higher-order thinking is used. Analyzing word choice is a critical higher-order thinking skill.

5. **Analyze the structure of texts, including how specific sentences, paragraphs, and larger portions of the text (e.g., a section, chapter, scene, or stanza) relate to each other and the whole.** When students have to think about the reason for the structure and organization of a text and how they relate to one another, then they are analyzing, which is a higher-order thinking skill.

6. **Assess how point of view or purpose shapes the content and style of a text.** When students are asked to look at how viewpoints or bias as well as purpose affect a text, they use higher-order thinking.

Integration of Knowledge and Ideas

7. **Integrate and evaluate content presented in diverse media formats, including visually and quantitatively, as well as in words.** As students evaluate and integrate information presented in different kinds of formats and seek to make connections between these diverse formats, they employ higher-order thinking.

8. **Delineate and evaluate the argument and specific claims in a text, including the validity of the reasoning as well as the relevance and sufficiency of the evidence.** Being able to argue and reason through a text requires that students use higher-order thinking.

9. **Analyze how two or more texts address similar themes or topics in order to build knowledge or to compare the approaches the authors take.** Comparing different texts to analyze the themes and the ways authors approach a text is higher-order thinking.

Anchor Standards for Writing

Text Types and Purposes

1. **Write arguments to support claims in an analysis of substantive topics or texts using valid reasoning and relevant and sufficient evidence.** Supporting claims through arguments is a hallmark of higher-order thinking.

2. **Write informative/explanatory texts to examine and convey complex ideas and information clearly and accurately through the effective selection, organization, and analysis of content.** Being able to examine, organize, and convey complex ideas requires higher-order thinking.

3. **Write narratives to develop real or imagined experiences or events using effective technique, well-chosen details, and well-structured event sequences.** This standard requires that students create text (be it real or imagined) that makes sense and flows. This level of creativity requires higher-order thinking.

Research to Build and Present Knowledge

4. **Gather relevant information from multiple print and digital sources, assess the credibility and accuracy of each source, and integrate the information while avoiding plagiarism.** To be able to assess the credibility and accuracy of a source requires students to think on higher levels. They are no longer just accepting facts given to them, they are deciding if these "facts" are accurate and credible as they produce texts that effectively summarize and present information using their own words.

5. **Draw evidence from literary or informational texts to support analysis, reflection, and research.** When students look for evidence to support their work—be it an analysis, a reflection, or personal research—they have to use higher-order thinking.

Anchor Standards for Speaking and Listening

Comprehension and Collaboration

1. **Prepare for and participate effectively in a range of conversations and collaborations with diverse partners, building on others' ideas and expressing their own clearly and persuasively.** Being able to build on others' ideas and to persuasively communicate these ideas demands higher-order thinking as students combine, build upon, and communicate in a persuasive manner.

2. **Integrate and evaluate information presented in diverse media and formats, including visually, quantitatively, and orally.** Evaluating information from diverse formats requires higher-order thinking as students have to make judgments and figure out how the information ties together.

3. **Evaluate a speaker's point of view, reasoning, and use of evidence and rhetoric.** To evaluate point of view and how a speaker uses word choice and sound evidence to make clear, well-developed claims/arguments necessitates higher-order thinking.

Presentation of Knowledge and Ideas

4. **Make strategic use of digital media and visual displays of data to express information and enhance understanding of presentations.** To be strategic about the use of media and visuals to effectively present information requires that students employ higher-order thinking.

5. **Adapt speech to a variety of contexts and communicative tasks, demonstrating command of formal English when indicated or appropriate.** Being able to adapt to different contexts and knowing what is appropriate within each one requires that students analyze the situations and make judgment calls.

Anchor Standards for Language

Vocabulary Acquisition and Use

1. **Determine or clarify the meaning of unknown and multiple-meaning words and phrases by using context clues, analyzing meaningful word parts, and consulting general and specialized reference materials, as appropriate.** Analyzing meaningful word parts and using context clues to determine the meaning of words require that students engage in higher-order thinking.

2. **Demonstrate understanding of figurative language, word relationships, and nuances in word meanings.** Reaching beyond the understanding of words to determine figurative language and how words relate to one another as well as interpreting word nuances necessitates more than just finding out what the words mean. It means that students have to look deep into the text and analyze these meanings, again requiring higher-order thinking.

These examples show that 21 out of the 32 total anchor standards specifically require the use of higher-order thinking to meet the standards. This examination of the anchor standards clearly demonstrates, more than anything, that teachers must design rigorous tasks for students that require deep thinking across multiple standards. One powerful way to do that is by using questioning strategies based on higher-order thinking.

What Are HOT Questions?

Questions that demand higher-order thinking (HOT) are those that invoke deep thinking rather than just a quick recall, comprehension, or application answer. Higher-order questions typically can have more than one correct answer, too. Examples of questions that are not higher-order in nature ask students to recall information, show what they learned, describe a character, list the items, and apply what they've learned. The answers students give are more or less finite and often on a literal level. These types of questions are efficient for quick formative assessments so the teacher knows when to move on to new content or reteach the present content. But, they are not useful for engaging in deep thinking.

> Questions that demand higher-order thinking are those that invoke deep thinking rather than just a quick recall, comprehension, or application answer. Higher-order questions typically can have more than one correct answer, too.

Open-ended questions (*What are the most important qualities a leader should possess?*), analysis questions (*What evidence can you find to support the author's claim that Charlotte acted as a savior for Wilbur?*), evaluative questions (*How would you justify the view that all princesses are spoiled?*), what-if questions (*What if the sky were red instead of blue?*), and creative questions (*How could you change the setting of Cinderella to give it a new twist?*) are a few examples of higher-order questions. Not all of these types of higher-order questions are demanded in the CCSS.

Importance of Text-Dependent Questions

To meet the CCSS, many of the higher-order questions must be text dependent. In the past, many teachers have seen the need for text-dependent questions, but many of these text-dependent questions required only lower-level thinking. For example, *Where in the text does it talk about the boys' experience at school?* This type of example has students going back to the text to find the answer, but it is a fact-based question that does not require higher-order thinking.

Now, the key in forming text-dependent questions is to make them higher-level questions, too. Why? The standards are not concerned with students discussing their personal connections to text or sharing their own opinions outside of the text boundaries. Instead, the standards focus on developing students' ability to develop opinions and then support those arguments based on solid evidence found in the text. The goal is to create responsive readers and thinkers.

Consider the following example of higher-order questions based on *Charlotte's Web* by E.B. White. Which question below is text-dependent?

Example 1: How would the story change if the setting were in New York City instead of on Zuckerman's farm?

Example 2: What do the text clues tell you about Charlotte's character? Why do you think that?

Both of these examples are higher-order questions, but Example 2 is a text-dependent higher-order question.

The step to making questions both higher-order and text-dependent begins with making a question a higher-order question first. Then, work on it to make it text dependent. For example, we took this question: *Who would be an ideal friend for Charlotte?* and worked on it until we could make it text dependent: *Based on what you know about Charlotte, create a character that would be an ideal friend for her. Use the evidence from the book to explain your decisions.* Students have to take what they have learned about Charlotte from the story and then explain their decisions using the text. As a result, we are asking students to form a text-dependent answer.

Another example comes from the reading of a picture book based on the original Brothers Grimm fairy tale titled *The Frog Prince* by Edith Tarcov and James Marshall. During a workshop, one group of teachers devised a set of higher-order questions that could be used with students of all ages that included: *How does this book show bias against princesses?* and *Use text evidence to dispute the statement that "they lived happily ever after."* All the examples listed here are open-ended questions, but as long as students can defend their answers with references to the text, then the questions meet the demands of the CCSS. Using sentence stems like the following is one way to make sure students are supporting their answers to higher-order questions with references to the text:

Ideas for Supporting Text-Dependent Responses

Put a sticky note on the pages that show your thinking about . . .

Show me the part in the text that supports . . . .

Use text evidence to tell why . . . .

I think _____ because in the text it states (says) . . . .

Based on these events/facts in the text, I think . . . .

The text clues that make me infer _____ are . . . .

Questioning strategies offer perfect venues for sparking deep thinking. Higher-order thinking won't just naturally occur if students are not given opportunities for it. By carefully crafting questions that nudge students to think "between the lines" about text, teachers can provide opportunities for students to employ higher-order thinking skills using content-area texts as well as literary texts. Asking higher-order questions within the subject matter benefits students because it enhances their learning *and* it increases their achievement within that subject matter (Beyer 1987).

Frameworks for Higher-Order Questions

For many years, teachers have used Bloom's Taxonomy as a framework for categorizing questions. Analyzing, creating, and evaluating are frequently used to describe higher-order thinking. The levels of thinking are differentiated by the complexity of the verbs.

Depth of Knowledge (DOK) is a scale of cognitive demand with four levels adapted from the work of Norman Webb at the University of Wisconsin. The levels of thinking are differentiated by the complexity of mental processing required.

The four levels of thinking are as follows:

Level 1 is described as the *recall level*, where facts, information, or procedures are recalled. It requires the lowest level of thinking.

Level 2 is defined as the *skill* or *concept level*. Typically, students classify, organize, estimate, collect, display, observe, and compare data. Students use the information they know. This level requires deeper thinking than does Level 1.

Level 3 is characterized by *strategic thinking*. Reasoning, planning, and making conjectures are typical of this level. Higher-order thinking comes into play when students have to defend the reason for selecting their answers. Students draw conclusions, support their conclusions with evidence, and then determine which concept to apply to solve a problem.

Level 4 is categorized by *extended thinking* and is the highest level of thinking with complex reasoning where students make interdisciplinary connections. Many activities at this level are performance-based tasks and can take extended periods of time.

Depth of Knowledge (DOK) does not depend on the complexity of the verb to make the question more complex, as Bloom's Taxonomy does. Instead of being driven by verbs, Depth of Knowledge is driven by complexity of the task. Notice that many of the following verbs would be listed at lower levels of thinking according to Bloom's Taxonomy: *explain, describe, identify,* and *tell.* But when using Depth of Knowledge as a framework, these verbs have very little or no determination on the complexity of task. While we love using the higher level of Bloom's verbs to ensure complex questions, for the Depth of Knowledge inquiry design example shown in Figure 4.1, using the lower level verbs makes sense. Since these verbs can be utilized across the first three levels of DOK, it is easier to demonstrate how a task's complexity changes when using the knowledge and comprehension of Bloom's level verbs. You will notice that the examples following are stated as inquiries. However, these inquiries can be easily framed as questions by using a sentence starter such as: *How can you…?* In the stair step visual seen here, you will see that there are four examples—one for a poem, one for an information science text, one for a fictional narrative story, and one for an informational social studies text or biography.

Figure 4.1 Depth of Knowledge Inquiry Design

	Level 3	• <u>Explain</u> how John Brown can be viewed as both a revolutionary and an insurgent. Support your answer with evidence from several sources. • <u>Describe</u> how the character came to think and act this way at the end of the story. Use situations and examples from the story to support your thinking. • <u>Identify</u> what would happen if snakes as predators, did not exist in an ecosystem. Use data to support your answers. • <u>Tell</u> why Frost would have written his poem "Nothing Gold Can Stay." Use information from several sources to defend your answer.
	Level 2	• <u>Explain</u> how people perceive John Brown's actions today. • <u>Describe</u> how the character is similar and different from another character in the story. • <u>Identify</u> why it is important to have predators in an ecosystem. • <u>Tell</u> why Frost used the analogy of Eden in his poem "Nothing Gold Can Stay."
Level 1		• <u>Explain</u> John Brown's antislavery views. • <u>Describe</u> the main character in the story. • <u>Identify</u> the important predators in an ecosystem. • <u>Tell</u> some of the ways that Frost referred to nature in the poem "Nothing Gold Can Stay."

Notice that each successive level takes the inquiry a step further up the ladder and requires deeper thinking from the students. The design of the Depth of Knowledge model portrays the increase of complexity at each level. Each inquiry frames how "high" a student will need to "jump" in their thinking to successfully respond. To effectively use the DOK levels to plan instruction, teachers should create inquiries that consider students' readiness in order to purposefully scaffold all students into the more complex Level 3 inquiries and questions. One interesting way to support students as they push into higher-order thinking is to begin with a Level 1 inquiry and then build upon the students' responses to nudge their thinking into a Level 3 inquiry that builds upon their previous thinking and responses. Notice also with each level, the students must defend their answers by referencing the text. While leveled questions and inquiries may sometimes be creative in nature, students' responses to these must also rest on evidence from the text as per the intent of the CCSS.

Higher-order questions work well for Level 3 in this framework. Level 3 thinkers assess, critique, hypothesize, cite evidence, investigate, draw conclusions, develop logical arguments, construct, and differentiate (Conklin 2012). For Level 3, virtually any verb can be used, such as those reflected in the higher levels of Bloom's Taxonomy, but the depth of thinking is key to defining the complexity of Depth of Knowledge Level 3. Let's more closely analyze the following example.

Level 1—Explain John Brown's antislavery views. This question is a basic fact-based question that does not require higher-level thinking.

Level 2—Explain how people perceive John Brown's actions today. This question involves students gathering information, but students do not have to use higher-level thinking to answer it.

Level 3—Explain how John Brown can be viewed as both a revolutionary and an insurgent. Support your answer with evidence from several sources. This question does require higher-order thinking because two polar opposite views of John Brown are presented. Students must come to terms with the controversial nature of this person with their answer, which is also text dependent.

The following chart shows some sentence stems that can be used to achieve Level 3 text-dependent questions.

Level 3 Text-Dependent Question Stems:

1. What kind of argument could you make to support _____? Be sure to show references to the text in your answer.

2. What kinds of conclusions could you draw about _____ based on what you read in the text?

3. How would you assess _____ based on what the text says?

4. What kinds of evidence would you cite to support _____?

5. What hypothesis would you create based on the information in the text?

6. How would you critique the point of view of _____? Support your answers with references to the text.

7. What kind of bias do you notice in the text about _____?

8. What do you infer about _____? Why? Show your reasons with references to the text.

A Framework for Reading Questions

When performing a close read with students, higher-order questions can provide the opportunity for real, significant, and engaging discussions. We use the word "real" because these questions foster discussion that seems to "grow up" and mimic how we would talk during a book club. The questions that are asked bring about deeper perceptions as students create text meaning and explore more sophisticated ideas such as theme, symbolism, and author's claims and biases. When the teacher has set clear expectations and modeled how to have effective cognitive, collaborative conversations, *and* students have had multiple experiences in sharing their ideas and thoughts in a risk-free, carefully structured environment that supports students' interactions with text and conversations with one another, the discussion protocol changes. No longer do we begin discussions with basic questions such as *Who was the main character?* Instead, we turn the discussion of general, key understandings of what was read over to the students by asking them to respond to the text with a question like *What are you thinking about this story? What do you think was significant in this text? Why?* Students then engage first with each other, discussing the text in small groups or with a partner. As we walk about dropping in on group conversations, if we see that students have confusions or do not understand the basic structure or ideas of the text, then we can "prime the pump" by asking a few basic fact-based questions that direct students back to the text for some of the significant details. After allowing students to respond to an initial, more open-ended question, the teacher can ask students to share their own higher-order questions about the text or the teacher can frame the types of questions that initiate a significant discussion about the deeper meanings within the text.

> No longer do we begin discussions with basic questions such as Who was the main character? Instead, we turn the discussion of general, key understandings of what was read over to the students by asking them to respond to the text with a question like What are you thinking about this story? What do you think was significant in this text? Why?

The example questions on the following pages show many Level 3 questions based on the framework of the anchor standards for reading. A teacher would pick and choose from the questions across repeated readings based on students' responses and demonstration of their level of understanding.

Elementary Example

More Than Anything Else by Marie Bradby

Key Ideas and Details (Reading Anchor Standards 1, 2, and 3)

1. From the story, the reader can conclude that Booker's family was poor. Find evidence from the text to support this conclusion.

2. What is the setting of the story? What evidence does the text provide? *(In this question, the students must use multiple pages—illustrations, and text—to infer the time and general place of the setting.)*

3. How did the setting/historic context impact Booker's dream of learning to read?

4. What was the influence of Booker's mother and the newspaperman in the story?

Vocabulary Acquisition and Use (Language Anchor Standards 4 and 5)

5. What does it mean when the main character says, "…my hunger is racing as fast as my heart"?

6. What does Booker imply when he says that he has jumped into another world and he is saved? Is this analogy powerful? Why or why not?

7. *Persistent* is a good character trait to describe Booker. Give evidence from the text to support how Booker demonstrates this trait.

Craft and Structure (Reading Anchor Standards 4 and 6)

8. Which details were critical to move the story forward to its conclusion?

9. The frog in the story is a symbol. What does the frog symbolize?

10. How does this symbol reflect Booker's life during this time period in history?

11. The story is written in first person. What is the impact of the first person point of view on the reader?

12. What do you think is the author's intended message in writing this text? Justify your thinking using text evidence.

Integration of Knowledge and Ideas (Intertextuality) (Reading Anchor Standards 7, 8, and 9)

13. How do you know that the author of *More Than Anything Else* knew about the actual life of Booker T. Washington? How did Booker's early experiences shape his life? Give text evidence from several sources to support your thinking.

(Show *Thank You, Mr. Falker* by Patricia Polacco and *The Hard Times Jar* by Ethel Footman Smothers.)

14. How are these three texts the same? How are they different?

15. Which character traits make Booker and Patricia Polacco's character in *Thank You, Mr. Falker* the same? How are they different?

16. What do the characters and events in *More Than Anything Else* and *The Hard-Times Jar* tell us about perseverance? Why do you think that?

17. (Show a video clip about the book.) How does the video clip portray the main character? How might the video make someone want to read this book or see this movie? Based on your reading, what would you add to the clip to make it more effective?

Grades 4-5 Example

Where Does Your Money Go? Time For Kids (Informational Text)

Key Ideas and Details (Reading Anchor Standards 1 and 2)

1. Based on what you read about wants and needs on page 26–27, reflect on the ways people spend money on pages 24–25. Which of these expenses would be considered needs? Wants? Why do you think this?

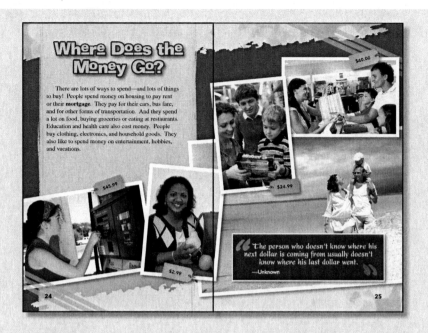

2. How might using coupons impact a family budget? Give examples based on text evidence. Could coupons ever actually "hurt" a family's budget? How?

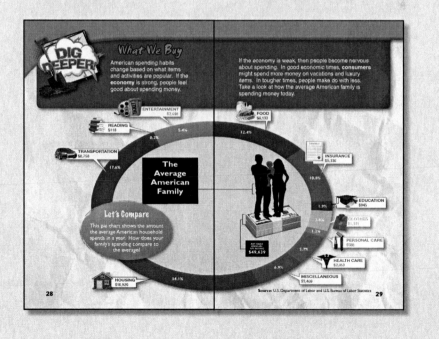

Vocabulary Acquisition and Use

3. What text evidence helps the reader understand the meaning of *consumer* on page 29?

Key Ideas and Details

4. What is the purpose of the text feature on these pages? What conclusions can you make about American families as consumers? What factors might change the information on this text feature? Consider what you have read in the previous pages.

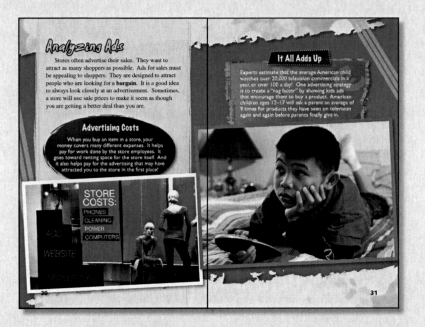

Craft and Structure (Reading Anchor Standard 6)

5. Do you think it is fair to use sale prices to make it seem as if people are getting a better deal than they are? Why or why not? Use the text to support your claim!

6. How might your feelings about using the "nag factor" change if you were a child? A parent? An advertiser?

Integration of Knowledge and Ideas (Intertextuality) (Reading Anchor Standards 7 and 8)

7. What kind of graphic organizer/thinking map could you create to show how advertisers design ads to influence your thinking? Use the text to support your thinking.

8. Select an advertisement. Are there any opinion-based features used that could be added to your graphic organizer/thinking map? Which ones? Why?

9. Now select at least two different advertisements. Using your graphic organizers, analyze what the advertisers did to attract shoppers.

Grades 6–8 Example

"Priscilla and the Wimps" by Richard Peck

Key Ideas and Details

1. From the story, the reader can conclude that the season of year is winter. Find evidence to support this conclusion.

2. Why did the narrator say that the only force stronger than Priscilla is fate? What did he mean by this?

3. How is Priscilla the perfect, and yet unexpected, hero of this story?

Vocabulary Acquisition and Use (Language Anchor Standards 4 and 5)

4. What does it mean when the narrator says, "Monk ran a tight ship"?

5. What does the narrator mean when he says that Priscilla was "... beautiful, in a bionic way"?

6. What does the narrator mean when he says, "Picture a girl named Priscilla Roseberry, and you would be light-years off"?

7. *Self-confident* is a good character trait to describe Priscilla. Give evidence from the text to support how Priscilla demonstrates this trait.

Craft and Structure (Reading Anchor Standards 4 and 5)

8. Which details were critical to move the story forward to its conclusion?

9. The school is compared to the Garden of Eden. What does the author mean by that?

10. In what ways does the author use the symbol of snakes in the story? Is this effective? Why or why not?

11. What is the impact of the first person point of view on the reader?

12. What do you think is the author's intended message in writing this text? Justify your thinking using text evidence.

Integration of Knowledge and Ideas (Intertextuality) (Reading Anchor Standards 7, 8, and 9)

13. How do you know that the author of "Priscilla and the Wimps" understood the realities of middle school life? What kinds of experiences would he have needed? Give text evidence from several sources to support your thinking.

14. How are these texts the same? How are they different?

15. Which character traits make Monk and Jeff Kinney's character Rodrick in *Diary of a Wimpy Kid, The Ugly Truth* the same? How are they different?

16. What do the characters and events in "Priscilla and the Wimps" and *Holes* tell us about friendship? Why do you think that?

17. How does this video clip portray the characters? How might the video make someone want to read this story or see this movie? Based on your reading, what would you add to the clip to make it more effective?

Grades 9–12 Example

Slavery in America, "Runaway Slave Poster"

Key Ideas/Details (Reading Anchor Standards 1, 2, and 3)

1. What are some of the unusual things you noticed about this poster? What are you thinking about the poster?

2. How is Dolly described? What do we know about her family?

3. What clues tell you about Dolly's life as a slave?

4. What does Dolly's owner think about Dolly? Explain your thinking using evidence from the poster.

Vocabulary Acquisition and Use (Language Anchor Standards 4 and 5)

5. What does it mean when the text says she (Dolly) is not a "very healthy person" while the poster also says that she has a "fine set of teeth"?

6. What could the phrase *enticed off* mean in this context?

Craft and Structure (Reading Anchor Standards 5 and 6)

7. How do we know that this document is historically important?

8. The intended purpose of this poster is to bring this runaway slave back to her family. How do we know this?

9. Why do you think the owner would blame the disappearance on being *enticed off*? Why wouldn't she run away instead?

Integration of Knowledge and Ideas (Reading Anchor Standards 7, 8, and 9)

(Responses will be based on text evidence from the poster along with several selected primary sources/text excerpts on the related time period.)

10. This poster was produced in 1863. What was happening in U.S. history in 1863?

11. What does the poster tell us about the people and events during the time in which it was created?

12. How can you use the poster and related texts to support the idea that laws have to change before people's minds will change?

13. In what ways do these texts tell Dolly's story?

14. What leads you to believe that Dolly wanted freedom—whether she really acted on it or not? Cite text evidence from these selected primary sources to support your thinking.

15. In what ways do these primary sources give us glimpses into the mindsets of the people during the times in which the texts were created?

When forming your own questions using the CCSS Anchors during a reading selection, use the examples listed previously and the stems in Figure 4.2 to help you form higher-order, text-dependent questions.

Figure 4.2 Forming Higher-Order, Text-Dependent Questions

Anchors	Question Stems	Text Evidence Stems
Key Ideas and Details	How might using _____ impact _____? Give examples based on text evidence. Could _____ ever actually "hurt" _____? How? What are some of the unusual things you noticed about _____? What are you thinking about this? From the story, the reader can conclude _____. Find evidence to support this conclusion. Why did the narrator say _____? What did he mean by this? What is the purpose of the text feature on these pages? What conclusions can you make about _____? What factors might change the information on this text feature? Consider what you have read in the previous pages.	Give evidence from the text to support _____. Justify your thinking using text evidence. Give text evidence from several sources to support your thinking. Give examples based on text evidence. Find evidence to support this conclusion.
Vocabulary Acquisition and Use	What does it mean when the narrator says _____? What could the phrase "_____" mean in this context? What text evidence helps the reader understand the meaning of _____ on page _____? _____ is a good character trait to describe the main character. Give evidence from the text to support this trait. What does the character imply when he says _____?	What text evidence helps the reader understand _____? Use the text to support your claim. How can you use the text and related texts to support _____? Show me in the book.
Craft and Structure	Which details were critical to move the story forward to its conclusion? In what ways does the author use the symbol of _____ in the story? Is this effective? Why or why not? What is the impact of the first person point of view on the reader? Do you think it is fair to _____? Why or why not? Use the text to support your claim. What do you think is the author's intended message in writing this text? Justify your thinking using text evidence.	Use the book to tell why. Support your answer with references to the text. Based on events in the story, _____? Put a sticky note on the pages that show your thinking about _____.
Integration of Knowledge and Ideas (Intertextuality)	How do we know that this document is historically important? How do you know that the author of _____ understood the _____? What kinds of experiences would he have needed? Give text evidence from several sources to support your thinking. How are these three texts the same? How are they different? Which character traits make _____ and _____ the same? How are they different? (Two different books) What do the characters and events in _____ and _____ tell us about friendship? Why do you think that? (Two different books) How does the video clip portray the characters? How might the video make someone want to read this story or see this movie? Based on your reading, what would you add to the clip to make it more effective? What kind of graphic organizer/thinking map could you create to show _____? What does the poster tell us about the people and events during the time in which it was created? In what ways do these texts tell _____ story? How can you use the text and related texts to support the idea that _____?	Show me the part in the text that supports _____. Use text evidence to tell why . . . . I think _____ because in the text it states (says) . . . . Based on these events/facts in the text, I think _____. The text clues that make me infer _____ are _____.

Performance-Based Tasks

Remember, the ultimate goal of close reading experiences is that the students eventually read and deeply comprehend text independently. Classroom close reading activities give teachers an approximation of where the students are in relation to independently processing the multiple layers of meaning called for by the CCSS. While teachers gather valuable data about their students during these kinds of group experiences, it is difficult to monitor student ownership of the process or individual student gains over time. This is where performance-based tasks come into the picture.

Performance-based tasks, completed at the independent level, are constructed to allow students to demonstrate what strategies they have "taken on" from close reading experiences, small group instruction, and other literacy contexts and can now apply on their own. The Smarter Balance Assessment Consortium (SBAC) describes performance tasks as tasks that challenge students to apply their knowledge and skills as they respond to complex, real-world problems. Stiggins, Arter, Chappuis, and Chappuis state that a performance-based assessment is an "assessment based on observation and judgment. Students engage in an activity that requires them to apply a performance skill or create a product and we judge its quality" (2004, 191). Performance tasks move beyond traditional assessments such as multiple-choice items to measure students' problem-solving and critical thinking skills. Not all of the standards lend themselves to measurement through a performance task, but because of the complex thinking and integrated strategies/skills set forth in the CCSS, a teacher will find that a performance task assessment can provide valid information on which to evaluate students' progress and make instructional decisions.

At its very heart, a performance-based task can engage students in multiple literacy activities, cover a variety of standards, and require students to "orchestrate" reading and comprehension strategies (Clay 1991) to successfully complete the task. A performance task based on a particular reading selection provides the opportunity for the teacher to analyze students' competencies in reading and comprehension, writing, language and word choice, and sentence or text structure, among other things. For example, in one task, students might analyze the text features and the significant main ideas of one text and then write about how those text features and main ideas compare to those found in another featured text. The Partnership for Assessment of Readiness for

College and Careers (PARCC) performance-based assessment design includes a focus on writing effectively when analyzing text. The SBAC links a theme or scenario to questions or activities that evaluate multiple student competencies such as deep understanding and analysis of text along with writing and research skills. Performance tasks that encompass literacy standards can also be utilized in the content areas.

Performance tasks are designed to carefully contextualize a task and appropriately articulate for the student the activities or engagements required. The performance task should also include explicit criteria that will be the basis of evaluating the students' performance on that task. Teachers may design checklists, rubrics, or even scoring proficiencies to use when observing and judging students' participation and product(s). We personally like involving students in the creation of the criteria at least to some extent in order to give the students "ownership" of the process and increase motivation. Although the performance task may be simple or complex, one important factor is that it must identify a clear and significant student focus or objective. The focus of the performance task is centered around the standards that you are ready to assess. The task itself will probably include some of the language of the standard(s) as to specifically identify for students the goal of the performance task (what will be measured). Note the example below from the CCSS, Appendix B, p. 93. The original text italicizes the language of the standard(s) assessed.

> *Although the performance task may be simple or complex, one important factor is that it must identify a clear and significant student focus or objective.*

Determine the *figurative and connotative meanings* of *words* such as *wayfaring, laconic,* and *taciturnity* as well as of *phrases* such as *hold his peace* in John Steinbeck's *Travels with Charley: In Search of America.* Then *analyze* how Steinbeck's *specific word choices* and diction impact the *meaning and tone* of his writing and the characterization of the individuals and places he describes. [RI.7.4]

Stiggins, et al. (2004), suggest considering the questions on the following page after selecting the focus/objectives.

1. What knowledge are the students to use?

2. What will the students perform or create?

3. What are the conditions that students adhere to for this task?

4. How much time will the students have for the task?

They also ask us to consider, "What will the criteria be for judging the performance or product?" We would add an additional question for the teacher: What materials/texts will the students need to complete the task? (Will the students need to locate any materials/texts on their own, or will these things be provided?)

We do not focus on performance-based tasks because they are the cornerstones of both the PARCC and SBAC proposed assessments. We give attention to these tasks because they are effective assessment tools that feed us valuable information so we know when and how we need to reteach and what new content or strategies the students are ready to add to their problem-solving analysis repertoire. We use performance-based tasks as formative assessment to drive our instruction and challenge individual students at the cusp of their learning potential.

> *A significant intent of the CCSS is to elevate students' thinking to the very highest levels so that they are prepared to enter the ever-so-competitive workplace in their futures.*

A significant intent of the CCSS is to elevate students' thinking to the very highest levels so that they are prepared to enter the ever-so-competitive workplace in their futures. Appendix B in the ELA standards contains exemplar performance tasks for each grade level related to the core standards. For example, examine these two sample performance tasks (one using literary texts and one using nonfiction text) based on the kindergarten standards. Notice the challenge of the performance level—what the students have to do to demonstrate proficiency.

"Students read two texts on the topic of pancakes (Tomie DePaola's *Pancakes for Breakfast* and Christina Rossetti's "Mix a Pancake") and distinguish between the text that is a *storybook* and the text that is a *poem*." [RL.K.5] (CCSS Appendix B, 28)

"Students (*with prompting and support from the teacher*) *describe the connection between* drag and flying in Fran Hodgkin's and True Kelley's *How People Learned to Fly* by performing the "arm spinning" experiment described in the text." [RI.K.3] (CCSS Appendix B, 36)

A teacher does not necessarily need to use these exact tasks; rather, the CCSS presents these as exemplars for us to use as models when designing tasks for our own students. The tasks we write should be at the level of complexity seen in the CCSS samples. When writing your own performance tasks, consider the level of understanding and critical thinking required of your students.

However, if you are just beginning to try out performance tasks with your students, you might start with selecting one of the sample CCSS tasks that assesses a standard (or standards) you have included in your instruction and are ready to see how your students can handle thinking on their own. Begin by reading the exemplar performance task with your students, and ask, "What are you being asked to do?" Then, walk your students through a process to deconstruct the task. Many students will not naturally be able to do this on their own. Often, the construction or length of the text within the performance task itself can be overwhelming when thinking about how to get started. We even felt this way after our first read of these examples from the 11th and 12th grade! (CCSS, Appendix B, 183)

"Students *integrate* the *information* provided by Mary C. Daly, vice president at the Federal Reserve Bank of San Francisco, with the data presented *visually* in the *FedViews* report. In their analysis of these *sources of information presented in diverse formats*, students frame and *address a question* or *solve a problem* raised by their *evaluation* of the evidence." [RH.11–12.7]

"Students *analyze* the concept of mass based on their close reading of Gordon Kane's "The Mysteries of Mass" and *cite specific textual evidence* from the *text* to answer the question of why elementary particles have mass at all. Students explain *important distinctions the author makes* regarding the Higgs field and the Higgs boson and their relationship to the concept of mass." [RST.11–12.1]

By explicitly teaching students to look at the performance task and identify the end product of that task, we help them be more successful in completing that task. Through multiple examples, we can support students by asking them to first find the task's end product—What do I have to tell/show/make/write/demonstrate? Underline the end goal within the task, or jot it down on a sticky note. Then, work through the performance task to identify the steps necessary to complete it by asking the students *How do I get there? What do I need to do to accomplish this?*

Using task analysis to break the performance task down into doable steps helps students find a starting point and then organize their thinking to complete the task. Supported task analysis is one way to differentiate the task for less-experienced readers who may need this scaffolding. Most students feel comfortable with performance tasks once they have made a "plan" for tackling it. One way to illustrate for students the possible steps or order necessary to complete the task might be to have them number a perceived order within the task's text, labeling what they need to do first, second, etc. Students can utilize any word clues within the performance task, such as *first, next, then*, or *finally*, in the same way. Some students like to jot down their own plan on a sticky note off to the side of the task. In these ways, the students learn to carefully read the task and break it into smaller steps to accomplish the goal. Although we want to "hand off" this deconstruction of the performance task to the students, you may find that some of your below-level readers may continue to need support in understanding the intent of the task. They can identify their first step, complete it independently, and then move on to the next step. The "work" of the performance task is still theirs to accomplish.

Let's look at the following example from the CCSS model performance tasks:

"Students *identify the overall structure of ideas, concepts, and information* in Seymour Simon's *Horses* (based on factors such as their speed and color) and *compare and* contrast that scheme to the one employed by Patricia Lauber in her book *Hurricanes: Earth's Mightiest Storms*." [RI.5.5] (CCSS Appendix B, 76)

Students must certainly employ higher-order thinking to successfully complete this task. So, what exactly is the task required in this example? Here, students are asked to compare and contrast the text structure that two authors employ in texts with two very different topics. What might the identified steps look like as the students "deconstruct" the performance task?

1. Read each text.

2. Look at several factors about horses and hurricanes that are the same, such as speed and color.

3. Identify the text structure in each text, and describe how each author presents his/her information.

4. Compare and contrast how the authors are the same and different in the presentation of their ideas and information.

5. Use _____ to show this comparison. (*The teacher can identify the vehicle for presenting their thinking, or the students can self-select their type of response. These responses could include a graphic organizer/thinking map, composition, an oral presentation, etc.*)

A teacher could require students to select a graphic organizer such as a Venn diagram or a T-chart or allow students to create their own graphic organizer to develop their response to the task. Or a teacher can offer students a different choice, such as writing and then presenting a newscast report for an evening news segment that explains the similarities and differences between the authors' style in presenting their topic. Additional ways to address the task might be to have students showcase their thinking by creating wiki pages comparing/contrasting the author's style and structure or by writing a comparative review of the books for a school website or a newspaper. The wiki pages and written reviews must target the parameters of the performance task.

Many of the CCSS exemplar tasks in Appendix B are focused on the analyzing, evaluating, and creating levels of Bloom's Taxonomy (Bloom 1956). Teachers engage students in explicit instruction about higher-level thinking so that they can better comprehend the intent of the performance task and the thinking that they will need to be successful with that task. Teachers expose students to the verbs often associated with multiple higher-level questions/tasks so they can identify higher-level questions/tasks and address them appropriately. Some teachers display the information on charts like Figure 4.3 to make students more aware of higher-order thinking "trigger words."

Teachers can also be quick to point out and praise students when they hear students raise higher-order questions in the classroom. When a teacher asks a question or assigns a task that demands thinking on the higher levels of Bloom's Taxonomy, students discuss how they might approach the question/task. Getting students to be aware of when higher-order thinking is called for is essential to keying students into their own metacognition as they work through a performance task.

Figure 4.3 Verbs Associated with Levels of Bloom's Taxonomy

Bloom's Taxonomy	Associated Verbs					
Analyzing	dissect	inspect	infer	categorize	discover	
	survey	examine	analyze	conclude		
Evaluating	award	criticize	justify	dispute	decide	recommend
	measure	assess	value	appraise	support	prove
Creating	elaborate	create	improve	design	modify	
	maximize	propose	change	adapt	originate	

So how might this consideration of verbs help students as they encounter a performance task? Read the 4th-5th grade performance task example below:

"Students *describe how the narrator's point of view* in Walter Farley's *The Black Stallion influences how events are described* and how the reader perceives the character of Alexander Ramsay, Jr." [RL.5.6] (CCSS Appendix B, 70)

First, look for the main verb. In this example, the verb is *describe*. Then, ask a question using that verb—*Describe what?* Your response might be, *Describe how the narrator's point of view influences the events and character.* Teachers can take the process a step further by encouraging students to write a question in their own words—*How does the narrator's point of view impact how the events are described and how the reader understands the character of Alexander?* This becomes an analysis-level question. As stated previously, the teacher may need to facilitate many conversations with students about this kind of processing before they can be independent, but that is the ultimate goal.

How to Write HOT Tasks

To provide students with the amount of practice they need with performance assessments, teachers will eventually need to write their own performance-based tasks. A different thinking model teachers can explore to develop performance tasks is Webb's Depth of Knowledge (DOK).

The Depth of Knowledge, Level 4, moves into the arena of performance-based tasks. Tasks at Level 4 are typically interdisciplinary and may take extended periods of time or class periods to complete. Many project-based learning and problem-based learning tasks qualify as higher-level, performance-based tasks and fall into the DOK Level 4 category.

Be aware that just because a project or task is assigned does not mean that task requires that students tap into higher-level thinking to complete it. For example, in an effort to be creative, a teacher might give this assignment: *Read the text "A Killer Quake in Asia" and retell the events in newscast format.* While this is a task that may have students exerting their creativity (a good thing!), it does not necessarily demand higher-order thinking because the task is simply to retell the text. With just a little tweaking, a teacher could assign the following: *Examine the text for author's point of view/bias, and then prepare a newscast summarizing the main points of the text from a different perspective.* This task taps into analytical thinking as well as being creative, and would qualify as a DOK Level 4 activity (Conklin 2012). It also exemplifies the type of thinking demanded by the CCSS.

Consider this example based on DOK Level 4. *In an original project, explain the possible thought processes that led to John Brown's actions and his ensuing impact on American history. Support your position with specific text evidence.* This is a performance-based activity, and it is also a higher-level task because students have to infer from multiple texts/primary sources what John Brown thought based on his actions and reactions to the events around him as evidenced in the texts read. The following is one example where a student took information from primary sources and other texts and showed John Brown's thoughts about the Dred Scott case.

Figure 4.4 Student Example #1 Based on DOK Level 4

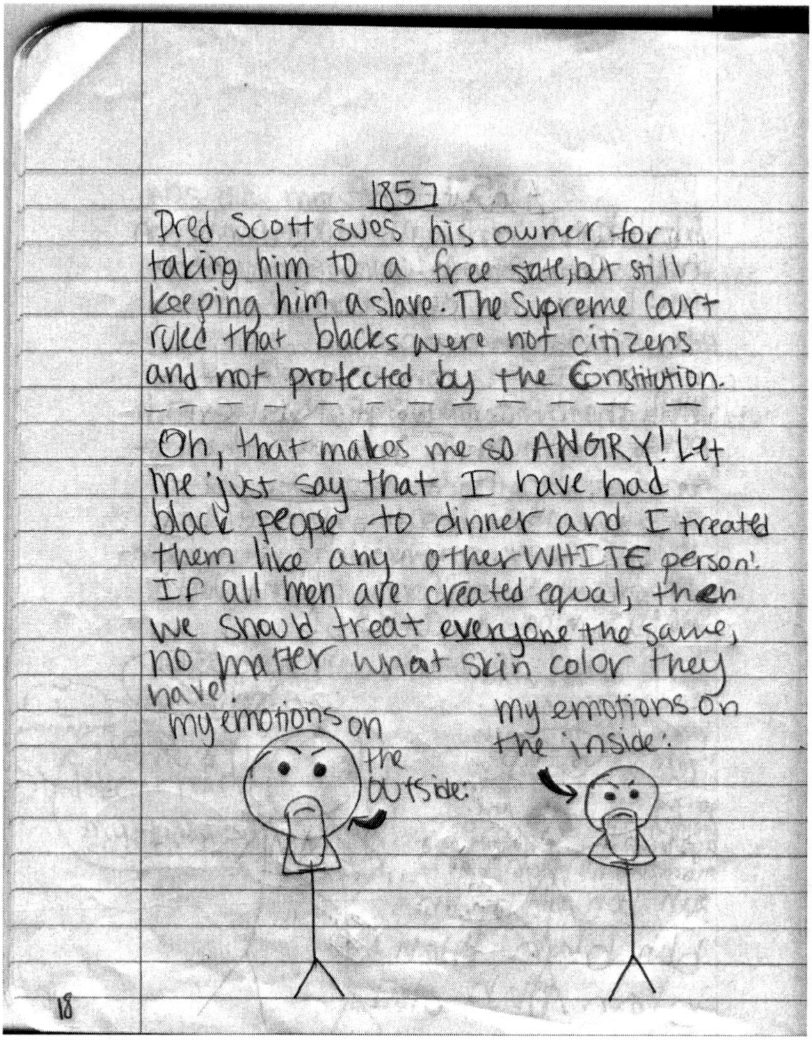

In the following high school example, a student created a comic strip about the forming of compounds in chemistry class based on a love story titled "As the Atoms Turn . . . A Story of Breakups, Bonding, and the Forming of New Compounds."

Figure 4.5 Student Example #2 Based on DOK Level 4

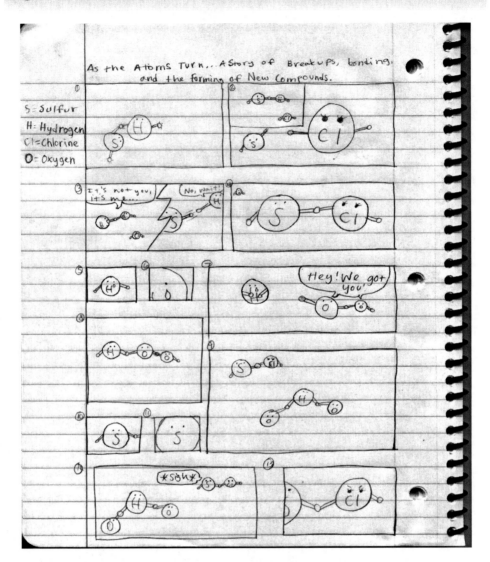

A key to constructing quality performance tasks is to be mindful of what you are asking students to do or produce. The thought demands should be centered on analyzing, evaluating, and creating (synthesizing). And, as an added bonus, we can often offer students a choice of venues to showcase their thinking. For example, instead of asking students to write their answers in an essay, you can offer several ways for students to present their responses. Keep in mind that the students are still accountable for the essentials of the task.

Their projects must reflect the performance criteria by which their work will be evaluated. Through sharing possible formats for "publishing" a response to a performance task, we establish what exceptional quality—or EQ—projects look like when students are given options.

- flipbooks
- trading cards
- bookmarks
- bumper stickers
- advertisements
- posters
- interviews
- brochures

- journal entries
- editorials
- letters
- newspaper articles
- videos
- web pages
- podcasts
- simulated social network pages

Using higher-order questions and tasks will give students the necessary practice for thinking deeper. Often teachers are surprised to learn that they do not have to throw out everything they have taught in the past. Rather, they just need to make small tweaks to those questions and tasks to make them higher-level. Finally, do not be afraid to offer these types of questions and tasks to all your students, even those who struggle with reading. All students, especially the struggling ones, need opportunities to think deeper. Remember, our students can think at much higher levels than we can even imagine if we just give them the opportunity to try.

Let's Think and Discuss

1. What level of DOK are the questions you predominately ask your students? What are some things you can do to immerse your students in higher-level thinking?

2. Consider how DOK can impact the performance-based tasks you design for your students. What can you do to ensure that these tasks challenge your students' higher-order thinking?

3. In what ways can you share the load with your teaching peers and work together to create your own higher-order questions and tasks?

Chapter 5

Close Reading in the Classroom

> *Close, analytic reading stresses engaging with a text of sufficient complexity directly and examining meaning thoroughly and methodically, encouraging students to read and reread deliberately. Directing student attention on the text itself empowers students to understand the central ideas and key supporting details. It also enables students to reflect on the meanings of individual words and sentences; the order in which sentences unfold; and the development of ideas over the course of the text, which ultimately leads students to arrive at an understanding of the text as a whole.*
> —Partnership for Assessment of Readiness for College and Careers 2001,7

Let's look inside a kindergarten classroom where the students have had many engaging conversations about literary and nonfiction texts in a risk-free environment. These students are comfortable sharing their thinking with the group as well as turning and talking about a text with a partner. The children have become quite proficient in retelling the important events in a story, including significant details from the beginning, middle, and end of the story. They have been working on "reading between the lines" to make inferences, and they have learned to support their thinking by returning to the text for "proof." Now, the teacher wants her students to focus on characterization by using text evidence from a story to infer how the main character thinks or feels on the inside. She wants the children to use a variety of words to describe the character in order to understand how the main character changes through the story. The teacher also wants to draw her students into focused conversations about the big ideas or themes in text and the author's writing craft. Therefore, this teacher creates a new close reading experience to engage her students in digging deeply into the meaning of a story.

The teacher selected the book *Widget* by Lyn Rossiter McFarland, a story about a little stray dog looking for a home. Widget discovers a house where Mrs. Diggs lives with her cats, "the girls." In order to fit in and be allowed to stay, Widget pretends that he is a cat. Although confused, the girls let Widget move in. Then one day, Mrs. Diggs falls and needs help, and only Widget can save the day by being a dog. The teacher does not frontload details or vocabulary from this book for the students with this first reading of *Widget*, but she reminds them to listen carefully to learn about the main character, Widget, the dog on the cover of the book, and what happens to him in the story so they can talk to their partner about the story after it is finished. After this first reading, the teacher invites the students to turn and talk to a partner about the story. Her students are accustomed to having this time to talk together about a text, and they enthusiastically jump into sharing their thoughts with each other. The teacher moves between the partnerships, prompting only when necessary with questions to support general understanding and pulling key details from the story such as *What did you think about_____ ? What happened then? What was important in the middle of the story? What surprised you in the story? What do you think about Widget as the main character? Why?*

The students next have the opportunity to share some of their comments with the whole group. Once again, the teacher prompts students with questions about key ideas from the story. The children especially love the humor behind Widget's cat-like behaviors, and they chat extensively about how hard he tried to fit into Mrs. Digg's home with the girls.

Today, the teacher is going to read the book a second time to the students. However, with this reading, the teacher plans to stop and "think aloud" about the character of Widget and how the text details can help the reader "read between the lines" to infer words to describe Widget. The students respond to prompts such as: *Tell me what you think. Why do you think that? What is your proof/evidence?* They then share their inferences using text evidence to support their thinking. The teacher pre-selects places in this new text where she will stop reading to have "cognitive conversations" with the students (see the Listening and Speaking Standards as well as the Reading Standards) about the text's meaning, vocabulary, and author's craft as they read between the lines using the text and illustrations in *Widget*.

The following conversation represents various students participating in the close reading conversation of Widget.

Teacher: When I read a story like Widget, I like to really look at the cover before I read to see if the author gives me any clues about the main character or what might happen in the story. (The teacher stops and lets the students make observations about the cover and the information it might provide the reader.) One of the things that the picture of Widget tells me is what he looks like on the outside. That will help me picture Widget in my mind as I read. Can you give me some words that describe Widget on the outside? I will write those words on this chart as you share your ideas.

Student: Big

Student: He is hairy—and fluffy.

Student: I think Widget is gray and white and black.

Student: Widget is dirty.

The teacher solicits about six to eight describing words.

Teacher: You gave some great describing words to tell all about how Widget looks on the outside so we would recognize him if we saw him. But as we read about a character in a story, we can also describe that character on the "inside"—how he thinks, what he feels like—and those "inside" describing words really help us understand that character and what he does or how he changes in the story.

Student: Yeah. Look at the cover. Widget looks surprised to see the cat shadow. His eyebrow is up like when you get surprised.

Teacher: Exactly. Surprised is a wonderful word to describe Widget on the "inside." I like the way that you used details from the text to support your thinking. That is what good readers do!

Teacher: Let's read the first page and carefully look at the illustration because we are doing a close reading of this story. (Teacher reads the first page.) Hm-m-m . . . this story begins with Widget walking down the road. He is a stray dog. How does the author help us know what stray means? Let's read that page again to look for clues. What do you think?

Student: It says that he has no home.

Student: It says that he had no friends. Poor Widget!

Student: Look! In the picture, he is all by himself. I bet he is feeling sad.

Teacher: So what do we think stray means?

Student: Stray means that you are all by yourself, and you have no home. You have nobody to take care of you.

Teacher: Great thinking, everyone! You used text clues and picture clues to help you figure out what stray means in this story. And someone even thought of the word sad to describe Widget on the "inside" from this first page. What is our proof for thinking that Widget was sad? Let's read between the lines. (Students share their thinking.)

Teacher: As we read, we are going to listen and look for story clues that will help us describe Widget on the inside so we can get to know him better. We will put those describing words with a sketch to help us read that word on our chart as we find our clues. So, right now, I will add the word sad to our chart to help describe Widget on the "inside" here at the beginning of our story. Let's read the next two pages. Think about words that we could use to describe Widget on the inside. (Teacher reads next two pages.) Turn and talk to your partner. What are words that you think describe Widget from these two pages? After, we will share our thinking.

Student: The author said that Widget was sad. See, we were right!

Teacher: Why did this page make you think that the author had picked a good word to describe Widget?

Student: Well, look at the picture. It is raining, and he had to hide in a log because he didn't have a house or any friends.

Student: He has a sad face, too.

Student: The words say that Widget was lonely. What does lonely mean?

Teacher: What do you think, boys and girls?

Student: I think lonely means that you don't have anybody to play with.

Student: You are all by yourself, and you wish you had a family or a friend.

Teacher: So, lonely means that you are all by yourself, and you wish that you had someone to be with. Poor Widget—he is feeling lonely. That word describes how he feels on the inside. Let's write that word with a sketch on our chart. So what words do we have to describe Widget so far?

Student: Sad! Lonely!

Teacher: *Now we will read a few pages before we stop and think.* (Teacher reads next five pages.) *Tell your partner what you are thinking about Widget now. I am wondering about what Mrs. Diggs means when she says that the girls just can't stand dogs.* (Students share with their partner and then a few share out with the group.)

Student: *I know the problem! Widget wants to stay at Mrs. Diggs's house so he won't be lonely, but the cats don't like him.*

Teacher: *Wow, you are really thinking about the story by telling us about Widget's problem! This makes the reader wonder what will happen next and read on to see if Widget will solve his problem.*

Student: *I think Widget is still sad because the girls don't like dogs, so they don't want him.*

Student: *I think he is mad because Mrs. Diggs would probably let him stay if she didn't have cats. I think she is sorry for him. I like dogs better than cats.*

Teacher: *Both of you are really thinking about how the details of the story and the pictures give us clues to read between the lines and figure out how Widget is feeling. We already have sad on our chart, so let's add the word mad.* (Teacher adds mad to the chart along with a sketch to support meaning.) *Let's read all the words that we have to describe Widget on the "inside" at the beginning of the story.* (The students read the words with the teacher.) *I like how we can make notes about our thinking as we read!*

Teacher: *Now we will read to see what happens in the middle of the story.* (Teacher reads the next twelve pages.) *Oh, my! What do you think about how Widget feels now?* (Students share their thinking with their partners, and then they discuss their ideas with the group.)

Student: *Yay! Now Widget is happy. He gets to stay at Mrs. Diggs' house. He has a home.*

Teacher: *Shall I write happy on our chart for a word that describes Widget in the middle of the story? Do we have evidence to prove that happy is a good word to use?*

Student: *Yes!*

Student: *I have a great word! I think Widget is excited.*

Teacher: *What happened in the story that makes you think that Widget is excited?*

Student: *He feels excited because he didn't have a home, but he fooled the cats. They think he is a cat.*

Student: *He is excited that his plan worked, and he can stay.*

Teacher: *So, boys and girls, do you think that we have enough proof to add excited to our chart?*

Student: Yes!

Teacher: *Can you share with your partner how Widget was able to get the girls to let him stay? (Students share.) Can I add a new word to our chart if I can find proof? The word that I would like to add is clever. Clever means that you are able to come up with good ideas to solve your problem. I think that Widget was clever because he did a lot of things to convince the girls that he was a cat. He was very smart to figure out a way to confuse the girls. Widget was clever. (The teacher writes the word clever on the chart and adds a sketch to support meaning.)*

Story Debrief

The teacher and students continue the close reading by reading the last two text chunks and add other "inside" words to describe Widget for the middle and the end of the story. See Figure 5.1 where the teacher recorded all of her students' thinking. At the end of the story, the teacher asked students to write one word (spelling the best that they could) that describes Widget at the end of the story and sketch that "inside" characterization word on a sticky note. They share their sticky notes and defend their choices with text proof.

Figure 5.1 Characterization Words Chart from *Widget*

To summarize this close reading time, the students retell the story using the characterization words on Figure 5.1. For example, *At the beginning of the story, Widget was sad and lonely because* _____ . Tomorrow, the teacher intends to have one more close reading experience with this text to dig into the text's themes and author's craft and relate this story to two other books with a similar theme that the students have read. See the teacher's plan for questions to address through the three-day close reading of *Widget*. Although she may not ask all the questions nor address them in order, this guide helps her integrate many of the CCSS for kindergarten reading.

Figure 5.2 Question Stems—Kindergarten

Anchor Standard Categories	Question Stems
Key Ideas and Details	What did you think about _____?
	What happened next?
	What was important in the middle of the story?
	What surprised you in the story? Why?
	What do you think about Widget as the main character? Why?
	Where did this story happen? How do you know?
	How did Widget get Mrs. Diggs to let him stay?
	Why did Widget decide to bark at the end of the story?
	What is Widget like on the "inside"? Which words best describe his character? Why? (This is also Standard 4 under Vocabulary Acquisition and Use.)
Vocabulary Acquisition and Use	What text clues did the book give us to help us know the meaning of *lonely*? *Clever* is a good word to describe Widget on the inside. Why?
	What does the author mean when he says that the "girls" were confused?
	Why is *content* a good word to describe Widget at the end of the story?
Craft and Structure	How did the author use humor to make this book fun to read?
	How is the book *Widget* different from a nonfiction book about dogs?
	What lesson do you think that the author wants to teach us in this book? (What did Widget learn? What did the "girls" learn?)
Integration of Knowledge and Ideas (Intertextuality)	How did the illustrations help us better understand the story?
	How is the character Widget like Gloria, the dog in *Officer Buckle and Gloria* by Peggy Rathmann? How is Widget different?

The level of expertise that these kindergarteners have already developed with understanding story elements, making inferences from text, and supporting their thinking with text evidence is probably amazing to teachers who work with older students. What would be even more amazing is what might happen if we consistently fostered this depth of thinking and "cognitive conversing" through the vehicle of close reading beginning in kindergarten. With the high expectations of the CCSS blossoming in the earliest grades, one can hardly imagine the complexity and independence of thinking that students might demonstrate during a close reading in middle school and beyond.

So what could a close reading of a text look like in a middle school classroom as students move into increasingly complex text using more sophisticated strategies to dig into the deep meaning within a text? In this example, the teacher chose not to frontload any plot details or vocabulary before the students read the text on their own. Now, let's drop in on the interactions between the teacher and a group of her ninth grade students after a first reading of "The Landlady" by Roald Dahl. There is a brief summary of the short story, and then what follows is an excerpt from the group's extended discussion.

With the high expectations of the CCSS blossoming in the earliest grades, one can hardly imagine the complexity and independence of thinking that students might demonstrate during a close reading in middle school and beyond.

Story Summary: "The Landlady" by Roald Dahl is a story about a young man named Billy who aspires to be a successful businessman. At just 17 years old, Billy lands a job with a company that sends him to a new town to begin work. On his way to a local hotel, a bed and breakfast sign catches his eye. The sign pulls him into the house where a strange landlady greets him. She was expecting him, or so she says. Billy is slow to realize the two previous tenants were murdered by the landlady and remain upstairs in the house, stuffed by an experienced taxidermist—the landlady.

(The following conversation represents various students participating in the close reading conversation of "The Landlady.")

Teacher: What are some unusual things you noticed about this story?

Student: I noticed the window that says "bed and breakfast." When he tries to go away, the sign makes him ring the doorbell and go inside.

Student: The whole situation of staying overnight was really cheap and convenient. Even the clothes on the bed—she knew he was going to be there. It seems too good to be true.

Student: I noticed that he was drawn to this house even though it was in a neighborhood that was run down.

Teacher: How do you know the neighborhood was run down? How did these details contribute to the tone or mood of the story?

Student: It said that the houses had paint chipping off. It also said the facades were blotchy from neglect.

Student: I noticed that the lady seemed creepy. She opened the door like a jack-in-the-box. There was no wait time.

Student: I noticed that she calls him by the wrong name twice. Once was Perkins and the other time Wilkins. I wondered why she did that.

Teacher: What does the text tell us about what Billy aspires to be?

Student: He wants to be a successful businessman and have an office. I know that because he talked about it. He has to go to bed early to get up and be at the office early.

Student: It's also in how he dresses. He wore a navy overcoat, brown suit, and brown hat. If he has to dress like that, then he probably has a good job.

Teacher: Does that surprise you? Why?

Student: A little bit, he is young. I wouldn't expect to see that now.

Student: He seems qualified for it. It was because of how he paid attention to the names in the book. He automatically thought that these looked familiar. He tried to figure it out. He pays attention to detail.

Student: Billy talks about walking briskly because all the successful men were brisk. The big shots at the office were brisk.

Teacher: *Tell me about Billy. Use the text to support your answers.*

Student: *Billy seems easy to control. He was drawn to the house by some force. Maybe that's how he got his job; his bosses can make him do what they want. He goes along with anything.*

Student: *I think he goes along because he is young, only 17 years old. He has a lack of experience as an adult. He acts in a naïve way.*

Teacher: *What did the text mean when it gave this description of a boardinghouse in Billy's mind:* watery cabbage, rapacious landladies, and a powerful smell of kippers in the living room?

Student: *I looked up kippers and it meant grilled fish.*

Student: **Rapacious** *looks like* **ravenous**. *I think it means someone who takes from others.*

Teacher: *What qualities did the landlady's perfect guests possess?*

Student: *They were young, handsome, undergraduates—good jobs, naïve, trusting.*

Teacher: *How did she know he was coming?*

Student: *She probably didn't really know he was coming, but she just said it to make him feel at home and welcomed.*

Student: *While she is creepy in how she looks at him, she still doesn't seem like a murderer.*

Teacher: *What do the red fingernails on white hands symbolize?*

Student: *They symbolize blood and death—how easily blood can show up on skin. We see that in Macbeth, too. The blood could not be washed from the hands.*

Teacher: *It seemed that Billy did remember the two men, even though he did not say everything aloud. Why did Billy not leave when he remembered the two men?*

Student: *I think it was something in his food that made him not act.*

Student: *The poison in his tea made him not leave. He didn't have any judgment. Remember the bitter almond taste?*

Student: *I think that he was too naïve to leave. The lady seemed strange to him, but harmless.*

Teacher: *What was the author trying to achieve in this story? Why do you think that?*

Student: *His message was to be more observant and have good judgment. Though Billy saw these things—he knew she was a taxidermist; no coats on the coat rack, but the men were still upstairs; the tea tasted weird. Still he did not leave.*

Student: *The last journal entry was two years ago. While Billy questioned that, he didn't leave.*

Student: *I agree. She talks about the two other guys in past tense, but she says they are still upstairs. Billy did not question it.*

Teacher: *(Students have viewed a movie of the short story, "The Landlady.") Compare the story to the movie. Why did it seem that the movie was more explicit? For example, the lady tells him he is going to die. It doesn't say that in the story.*

Student: *I think that written words have a way of showing. Even though the actions should be stronger than words, sometimes you have to say what is going to happen for the audience to get it.*

Student: *I don't think it needed to be more explicit. As was said, the actions of Billy and the landlady should be powerful enough to make the audience know what is going to happen. The movie would have been better without being so explicit. Let the audience read between the lines, you know?*

Story Debrief

This example reveals a portion of a close reading with a group of ninth grade students who have had many close reading experiences with a variety of texts. As these students engage in frequent close readings, they improve their deep analysis of text at multiple levels of meaning. They incorporate much of the academic vocabulary used in the text (and from other texts) into their discussions, and they offer thoughtful, provocative reflections and responses to questions. The students "piggyback" off of other's comments, support and/or defend their responses, and, together, negotiate meaning from the text. These students are less consumed with literal details and, instead, use the key details of text to support their inferences and analysis of the characters, plot, and author's craft. Notice how the teacher's "blueprint" or plan for the close reading structures the questions using the anchor standards as a guide (also discussed in the previous chapter).

Figure 5.3 Question Stems—Ninth Grade

Anchors	Question Examples
Key Ideas and Details	What are some unusual things you noticed about this story?
	What does the text tell us about what Billy aspires to be?
	Tell me about Billy. Use the text to support your answers.
	What qualities did the landlady's perfect guests possess?
Vocabulary Acquisition and Use	What did the text mean when it gave this description of a boardinghouse in Billy's mind: *watery cabbage, rapacious landladies, and a powerful smell of kippers in the living room*?
Craft and Structure	How did the landlady know Billy was coming?
	What do the red fingernails on white hands symbolize?
	It seemed that Billy did remember the two men, even though he did not say everything aloud. Why did Billy not leave when he remembered the two men?
	How does the author utilize foreshadowing in this story? Is it effective? Why or why not?
	What was the author trying to achieve in this story? Why do you think that?
Integration of Knowledge and Ideas (Intertextuality)	Compare and contrast the story to the movie: Why did it seem that the movie was more explicit? For example, in the movie, the landlady tells Billy that he is going to die, but it doesn't say that in the story. Which is more effective—the book or the movie? Why?

The last question extends students' thinking intertextually by asking them to compare and contrast the content and style/craft of what they read with a movie of the story. We want students to think beyond this story and to make connections rooted in the text and the movie content. One of the students even made his own intertextual comparison with his comment likening a part of "The Landlady" to the play, *Macbeth*. The teacher could extend that student's analogy and have students read the referenced *Macbeth* scene to understand how that text reference relates to "The Landlady."

Although the teacher's plan for this close reading provides the blueprint for the lesson, when appropriate, the teacher poses additional questions based on what the students actually said during the conversation about the text. In the following examples, the teacher follows up for depth of thinking, forcing students to defend their answers.

Example 1:

> **Student:** *It's also in how he dresses. He wore a navy overcoat, brown suit, and brown hat. If he has to dress like that, then he probably has a good job.*

> **Teacher:** *Does that surprise you? Why?*

Example 2:

> **Student:** *I noticed that he was drawn to this house, even though it was in a neighborhood that was run down.*

> **Teacher:** *How do you know the neighborhood was run down? How did these details contribute to the tone or mood of the story?*

As these students continue to develop analytic expertise as readers, this teacher may find that the students frequently drive the conversations about the text's meanings and realize that questions from her blueprint may have already been addressed by the students. She may also find that she can weave key questions into the discussion based on the comments of her students rather than the order in which she wrote the questions in her plan. This teacher's students are well on their way to developing the expertise required by the CCSS to process and analyze grade level complex text.

What Is a Close Reading?

A close reading is a sustained, careful examination of the deep meaning behind a short, complex text. The goal is to delve deeply into the text with the intention of teaching students how to handle such texts when reading independently. Often, close reading involves multiple readings of the same text to uncover the layers of meaning and explore the text's structure as well as the author's craft and language.

Teachers should not be intimidated by close reading. While there is some direction we need to take to have a successful close reading, the process is not so structured that we cannot make it work for our students. We, the teachers, should own this context for reading in our classrooms. Close reading is only one of the instructional contexts that we include in the day. Read-alouds, model lessons and think-alouds, small-group directed instruction, and independent reading and writing are equally essential for our students. In the end, close reading is about having authentic conversations about a text that demonstrate for students what they will take into their independent practice in reading.

> *We believe in what we call "an evolving understanding" of close reading. In other words, there doesn't have to be a rigid formula that we must adhere to in order to have a successful close reading experience with our students. Close reading leads to real conversations about text, and there is no age barrier on having these rich conversations.*

We believe in what we call "an evolving understanding" of close reading. In other words, there doesn't have to be a rigid formula that we must adhere to in order to have a successful close reading experience with our students. Close reading leads to real conversations about text, and there is no age barrier on having these rich conversations. "Young children benefit from opportunities to talk about the hazy feelings, ideas, and images they have during reading. Teachers need to provide plenty of time for children to talk about what they are thinking during reading. Through this talk, children can discover what they actually *do* think" (McGee 1995).

Beginning with our youngest readers, close reading of grade-level, complex text encompasses all readers, whether below-level, on-level, or above-level, in considering the big ideas and key supporting details, the language, the structure, and the development of ideas in a text. As teachers, we carefully plan the close reading time to ensure a successful experience for our students, scaffolding our support only when necessary to move the students forward into new realizations about the text. The following pages discuss the main points to consider for a close reading.

1. **Purposefully select a short grade level complex text or an excerpt of a longer text, fiction or nonfiction, that will challenge your students' thinking and provide them the opportunity to dig into a significant text**. As you plan, consider the CCSS that could be embedded in a close reading experience with that text. Using a short, powerful text allows you and your students to really delve into a grade-level, complex selection and not be overwhelmed by the amount of text or the time needed to engage with and process that text (Coleman and Pimentel 2012 and Fisher, Frey, and Lapp 2012). Also, using short texts in close reading sessions opens the door to providing students varied opportunities to deeply process texts across many different genres rather than spending too much time on just one longer text. It is important to keep in mind that "close reading is as much a way of thinking and processing text that is emphasized throughout the Common Core as it is about a way of reading a singular piece of text" (Brown and Kappes 2012, 2).

Note that not all texts are appropriate for close reading. Purpose for reading drives text selection for close reading, especially since all texts do not require the same level of focus to extract meaning. For example, we may read easy-to-understand books simply for enjoyment or skim a fashion magazine article just for the big ideas and latest trends. At other times, depending on our purpose, we really dig into a text and try to deeply analyze the meaning behind the words. For a close reading, teachers choose a significant text with multiple layers of meaning along with more sophisticated structures and language. In primary grade classrooms, many picture books (both fiction and nonfiction; see CCSS Appendix B for multiple examples) work well for a close reading experience.

With these books, the teacher can read aloud or share read the text with the students, thereby, through listening comprehension, giving students opportunities to build knowledge and work with more challenging text than they can probably yet read independently.

Some possible questions to consider when selecting texts for close reading include: *Why should I select this text, and what do I want students to come away with after this experience? Is this text complex and worth the time and attention necessary for a close reading? Does the text exemplify powerful author's craft, unique text structures, and/or varied academic vocabulary?*

Is the text critical for building understanding in the context of what I am teaching (for example, a close reading of the Declaration of Independence in an American history class)? The selection of a "good-fit," close reading text depends on your purpose, your instructional context, and the depth of understanding that you want your students to achieve through focused comprehension conversations about that text.

2. **Keep the frontloading or pre-teaching of the text to a minimum for a close reading** (Fisher, Frey, and Lapp 2012). Provide a purpose for reading, and create an atmosphere that engages students, but, in this instructional context, let the text be the "teacher" whenever possible.

3. **Make time for repeated readings of the text through close reading**. These repeated readings usually happen across several sessions/days with the text. With each reading, students dig deeper into the text, noticing new things and responding to different questions and considerations. Expect close reading to take time. This experience is *not* a quick 15-minute activity. Set aside approximately 20–30 minutes per session for students to read, reread, and interact with the same text. Brown and Kappes (2012, 2) explain, "Through text-based questions and discussion, students are guided to deeply analyze and appreciate various aspects of the text, such as key vocabulary and how its meaning is shaped by context; attention to form, tone, imagery, and/or rhetorical devices; the significance of word choice and syntax; and the discovery of different levels of meaning as passages are read multiple times."

4. **Write and ask higher-order, text-dependent questions to engage students in powerful conversations about the close reading text**. Create questions that "prime the pump" for students to dig out the deeper meanings from text. Move students beyond literal understanding to inferential, between-the-lines thinking about the text, requiring them to support their responses with text evidence. Remind students to keep their responses and comments grounded within the "four corners" of the text. When necessary, steer the conversation away from personal connections or wild tangents. Frame questions that address all of the anchor standards, including those on author's craft, text structure, and possible intertextual connections. As students become more active in close reading by sharing their thoughts about a text and negotiating meaning through group dialogue, expect that more and more quality,

high-level questions will come from them. With time and experience, increasingly independent, student-driven "cognitive conversations" about text will evolve (Fisher, Frey, and Lapp 2012; Boyles 2012).

5. **Provide opportunities during close reading for readers to respond to text through annotations that can focus students' attention on the text and be used to support their thinking during text discussions**. Model multiple ways that readers can jot down their thinking to note the big ideas, inferences, or questions they are considering. Strong annotations anchor the students to the text, providing examples of text evidence to return to when responding to questions/comments about the featured close reading selection. Annotations can include sketches or notes in the text margins or on sticky notes, arrow sticky notes, wiki sticks, or highlighter tape to use in big books for younger students, underlining, circling, or employing an agreed-upon system of text coding (example: ! = important idea, * = key point, I = inference). However, keep in mind that "meaning doesn't arrive because we have highlighted text or used sticky notes or written the right words on a comprehension worksheet. Meaning arrives because we purposefully engaged in thinking while we read" (Tovani 2004, 9).

Successful close reads begin with determining the complexity of a text. (See Chapter 3 to help you select appropriate complex texts for a close read.) Then, think about the instructional goals for your lesson. It is important to plan close reading with a clear understanding that multiple standards, such as vocabulary and text structure, will be addressed as will be reading comprehension. Students should be challenged to think deeply about the text, so reference our chapter on forming questions, and use the framework we provide to ensure that any close reading questions are high level and text dependent. Prepare a minimum of five questions that probe students' thinking, and check that some of your key ideas and detailed questions are also inferential questions. Even though you enter the close reading lesson with a plan and a possible set of questions, keep in mind that the goal is to shift the conversation and cognition to the students. Our goal is that our students become increasingly strategic and thoughtful about text while developing into proficient processors of meaning.

Close reading seamlessly weaves together good instructional support, moving students from independence to shared/interactive processing to responding to teachers as they think aloud or model strategies using the text. The close reading experience usually incorporates many anchor standards at the same time. It is important to understand that as you weave together a close reading, *you* are not the sole constructor of the conversation. The students are a big part of this. (See the Speaking and Listening Standards for your grade level.) Maria Nichols, in her book, *Talking About Text: Guiding Students to Increase Comprehension Through Purposeful Talk*, notes, "Purposeful talk is focused, collaborative talk; it is a social process that requires students to actively engage with ideas, think out loud together, and work to a co-construction of those ideas" (2009, 12).

Venture forth into a close reading with concrete ideas of what you want students to unearth from the text and bring into the light—be it figurative language and imagery, author's craft, text structure, author's point of view/bias, character, surface level theme, deeper theme, central ideas/critical supporting details, etc.

Venture forth into a close reading with concrete ideas of what you want students to unearth from the text and bring into the light—be it figurative language and imagery, author's craft, text structure, author's point of view/bias, character, surface level theme, deeper theme, central ideas/critical supporting details, etc. Then, as Marie Clay so aptly states, "follow the child," or student. Attend to what the students are saying and doing to adapt your instructional blueprint for the close reading. As the students respond to the text, you may need to reinforce their processing, scaffold their thinking, teach them something new about text, or prompt them to extend their responses, coaching them into where you want them to go with the text.

Why Do Close Reading?

It's the teacher's job to ensure that students move forward in their ability to comprehend increasingly complex text and delve beyond a surface understanding of a text. Close reading is one of the most effective ways to demonstrate what it looks like to actively engage in digging into the multiple layers of text meaning. "A significant body of research links the close reading of complex text—whether the student is a struggling reader or advanced—to significant gains in reading proficiency and finds close reading to be a key component of college and career readiness" (Partnership for Assessment of Readiness for College and Careers 2011, 7). In her article on close reading, Nancy Boyles notes that too often educators choose to wait until middle or high school before exposing students to close reading because older students tend to think abstractly with greater ease than elementary students and the demands of secondary reading require close analysis of text. However, all students, kindergarten through twelfth grade, should be participating in close reading to develop the habits of thinking that develop a deep understanding of text at every grade level (Boyles 2012).

The CCSS state, "Students can, without significant scaffolding, comprehend and evaluate complex texts across a range of types and disciplines, and they can construct effective arguments and convey intricate or multifaceted information" (2010, 7). Many teachers wonder how they will get all their students to meet this expectation when some of the students in their classrooms do not read grade level text. Here we state again that the close reading is not the only literacy context for readers each day. Our students, especially those reading below grade level, will have many opportunities daily to work with good-fit challenging text at their instructional level through small-group, directed instruction designed to accelerate students' reading levels and comprehension. In these groups, teachers can carefully monitor, prompt for, and reinforce sound reading behaviors/strategies at the cusp of the students' challenge level. The strategies and skills developed, practiced, and firmed up in these small group sessions as well as the strategic comprehension work and problem solving that students extend into their independent reading time will be the strengths that they carry into the close reading experience.

Remember, what the CCSS state here about reading and processing complex text is the *end goal*. To achieve this goal, we must closely read many, many, many texts with students. Teachers model this depth of thinking and extend opportunities for students to successfully respond to texts over and over again. A close reading exemplifies a true application of the gradual release of responsibility (Brown and Kappes 2012). The teacher fluidly orchestrates toward independent student processing of text through shared/interactive negotiations of meaning, guided practice of the anchor standards embedded in the experience, and even modeled think-alouds to demonstrate what good

readers do to construct meaning. Even wh
read the text, we have found by scaffolding
reading aloud, shared reading of the text, ⱡ
deeply about the text, often surprising us wit
inferences rooted in text evidence. With eⱥ
take over more of the reading process, exp
text such as theme, author's craft, and text st
is an essential experience for students of all
required by the CCSS.

Close reading, as seen through the lens ⱡ
formative assessment, provides us with a ric
harvest of data about our students—wher
they are as readers and where they need tⱱ
go next. It springboards us into action so we
are able to target students' instructional goals
utilizing different contexts, including model
lessons, shared/interactive practice, and
small instructional groups. Through all these
experiences, students learn to synthesize
multiple metacognitive strategies, which they
can then apply in their own independent
reading.

> formative assessment, provides us with a rich harvest of data about our students—where they are as readers and where they need to go next.

Think and Discuss

1. If you were the kindergarten teacher, after this close reading of *Widget*, where would you go next instructionally with these students? What would be your goal? Why?

2. After reading "The Landlady," what might the teacher need to do next? How or why would you make that determination?

3. Look back at the examples at the beginning of the chapter and tell why they are an example of a close reading.

Chapter 6

I Do and *We Do*—Modeled and Shared Interactive Strategy Use

> *A teacher's job is always to bridge from the known to the new. Because there really is no other choice. Kids are who they are. They know what they know. They bring what they bring. Our job is not to wish that students knew more or knew differently. Our job is to turn each student's knowledge, along with the diversity of knowledge we will encounter in a classroom of learners, into a curricular strength rather than an instructional inconvenience*
>
> —Pearson 1996, 273

In many classrooms today, teachers, who feel pressed by a schedule, with seemingly too many things to do and too little time, sometimes find themselves modeling a reading strategy or process for their students and then immediately turning this work over to the students to do on their own. These teachers recognize the critical need for a targeted think-aloud to demonstrate new learning for students. Thus, the teachers thoughtfully present a model lesson for their students. However, when this lesson gives way directly into students' independent application of what was just demonstrated, essential key components of scaffolding, based on good pedagogy and research, are eliminated. As a result, we find that many students struggle to skillfully carry forward the strategies and standards they are now expected to employ in their own reading.

The missing steps of scaffolded support in the previous scenario include shared/interactive engagements between the teacher and students as they "try on" the strategy focus of the model lesson together and the subsequent small group instructional practice groups where the students now "do" the strategy, yet remain up close and personal with the teacher, who serves as a guiding coach. A gradual release of responsibility plan (Pearson and Gallagher 1983) provides students with directed teacher support at the introductory onset of new strategy work and strong student control of that strategy at the end of instruction, enabling students to successfully negotiate and integrate into their own practice the rigorous expectations set forth in the CCSS. These standards are multidimensional and multifaceted, and teachers need a powerful instructional tool such as the gradual release of responsibility model in order to design instruction that challenges students without frustrating them as they actively integrate new learning and strategies into their personal practice across multiple contexts.

We delve into a better understanding of the gradual release of responsibility model by first examining the work of Lev Vygotsky. Vygotsky describes how we take on new learning through his Zone of Proximal Development (ZPD) concept. His insights on the personal construction of meaning through social interactions about cognition spread in the 1960s. Over the years, many researchers, psychologists, and educators have explored and expanded upon Vygotsky's theories about learning (Vygotsky 1962; Tharp and Gallimore 1988; Bodrova and Leong 1996; Lyons 2003).

Figure 6.1 Zone of Proximal Development

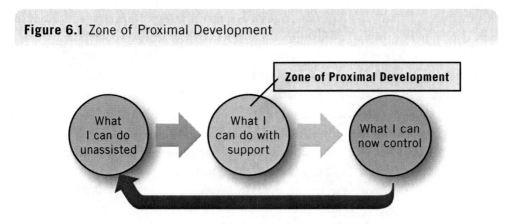

The zone represents a continuum of potential strategies or behaviors that are close to emerging and developing in the learner in the near future (proximal)

with assistance from someone more knowledgeable than the learner. The ZPD is fluid, recursive, and ever changing as a student moves from what he or she can do with assistance to independent action and then cycles back to taking on new learning with assistance. The ZPD represents the distance between what a student can do independently through personal processing and problem-solving and what the student can achieve through collaboration with and assistance from a more capable adult or peer. Tharp and Gallimore (1988, 33–39) build upon Vygotsky's theories by articulating several distinct phases or stages of the Zone of Proximal Development. As you read, consider the phases of the ZPD in the context of teaching your students a new reading strategy or standard.

As educators, we always begin with what students can do independently without support. Just as Pearson states in the opening quote, we bridge from the known to the new. Good assessment targets a student's "starting line." During the first phase of the ZPD, the teacher provides assistance to the students through specific cognitive language and demonstrations of what the strategy looks like and sounds like in action. The teacher scaffolds students into an understanding of the strategy and its application by making the role of the learner easier. This is done by providing assistance that gradually decreases as the learners take on more responsibility for the strategy (Wood, Bruner, and Ross 1976). The teacher, as the expert, helps students organize their thinking and learn the procedures necessary to eventually take the strategy into personal use. The teacher engages the students through meaningful dialogue, asking questions that probe the students' current level of understanding. The teacher invites students into the strategy work and strives to offer targeted feedback and clarify confusions as the students begin to dig into the process (Pearson and Gallagher 1983; Tharp and Gallimore 1988; Bodrova and Leong 1996).

> The teacher, as the expert, helps students organize their thinking and learn the procedures necessary to eventually take the strategy into personal use. The teacher engages the students through meaningful dialogue, asking questions that probe the students' current level of understanding.

In the second phase, the control for the strategy's application shifts to the students. The students begin to internalize the language of the strategy through collegial conversations and actually start to "rehearse" the strategy (shared, interactive practice). The students engage in "self-talk" as they problem-solve new reading challenges. The language of strategic processing and thinking provided to the students through the modeling and demonstrating phase begins to appear in the students' own musings and conversations about their reading. Students' metacognition—thinking out loud about their own thinking—gives teachers a window into the students' current level of processing and comprehending text. The teacher facilitates their evolving self-assistance by monitoring their thinking and actions as well as providing purposeful feedback. The teacher continues to prompt for the intended strategy or redirect the students as necessary to prevent the students from making the same processing or procedural errors over and over again. The students take on increasing personal control of their own learning using the strategy/standard.

The third phase of the ZPD finds the students taking on self-regulation of the strategy, maintaining individual control of and responsibility for the task. The students appear to internalize the strategy, and they use it with increasing flexibility and fluency. They no longer "talk out" their strategy use; rather, the reading work occurs in the readers' minds, becoming more efficient and effective as the students begin to "own" the strategy.

Next, in phase four, the students develop fluidity with the strategy, firming up the process until it is completely "known." With repeated practice, students display increased independence and flexible control of the strategy as they seamlessly integrate it into their strategic reading repertoire. Tharp and Gallimore (1988, 35) refer to this automatization of the strategy as "fossilized" performance. The students become strategically skilled participants in the reading (or any literacy) process, employing their internal cognition to plan, problem-solve, and proceed.

However, as teachers, we continually challenge our students with new learning goals and levels of understanding as we push toward the "what" of the CCSS. A final phase of the ZPD occurs when a strategy becomes "de-automatized" through the introduction of a more complex application of the strategy or the integration of a new strategic process. Students are forced to revert to an earlier stage of the ZPD to solve the problem. Some students may return to self-talk to negotiate the text, while other students may require more direct assistance from the teacher. Often, a new task adds a different "face" to previous strategy work because now that strategy must be applied in a new context. The teacher adjusts the scaffold to provide the least amount of support necessary to help the student address the challenge.

To continually accelerate students' learning, teachers intentionally create instructional conditions to recursively navigate students through the ZPD. As students recycle through the phases of the ZPD, they build ever-increasing reservoirs of procedural processes and cognitive networks, solidifying their "known" while taking on the "new." The intensity of support and the amount of time required during the first three phases of the ZPD varies from student to student. Ongoing assessment provides teachers with the necessary information to structure their "scaffolds" accordingly.

The gradual release of responsibility model provides the concept for a carefully structured instructional plan based on the phases of the ZPD. We believe that this scaffolding provides the critical pedagogical framework for our classrooms to help us design instruction that will support our students as they navigate and successfully achieve the high expectations of the CCSS whether we are looking at the ELA Standards or the Math Standards (or any other specified instructional standards). The teacher moves students through modeled demonstration of the strategy to shared interactive practice to guided practice and finally, to independent practice and flexible strategy use (Holdaway 1979; Pearson and Gallagher 1983; Tharp and Gallimore 1988). When instruction begins at the cusp of where students are currently as learners, these levels of classroom support are essential in helping students develop inner control of new strategies. Moving from the greatest level of teacher support to a minimal level of support ensures that students continually develop and incorporate new patterns for learning and creating meaning into their own literacy work.

> *Moving from the greatest level of teacher support to a minimal level of support ensures that students continually develop and incorporate new patterns for learning and creating meaning into their own literacy work.*

Once we carefully assess and determine what students currently control as learners, we are ready to move into what they need to know next. When teaching something new, there are four specific levels of teacher support that represent a release of responsibility to student independence:

1. Teacher control of the strategy through modeling and cognitive conversations with students

2. Shared, interactive engagement between the teacher and students using the strategy collaboratively

3. Guided practice of the strategy where the students take control while the teacher provides support, clarification, and feedback as needed

4. Independent application of the strategy by the students

(Pearson and Fielding 1991; Wilhelm 2001; Duke and Pearson 2002)

Figure 6.2 The Gradual Release of Responsibility Model

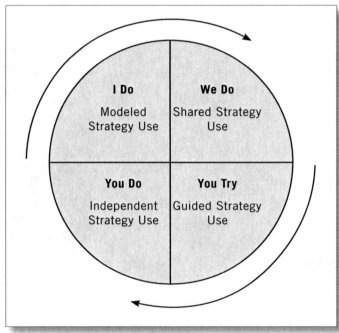

Understanding the *I Do*—Modeled Strategy Use

Often when we present to teachers, we say that this *I Do* level of gradual release in instruction is our "walk the walk, and talk the talk" time. While we are not sure who originally coined this sentiment, we do feel that it fits our goal. We want to model the actions ("the walk") and the thinking language ("the talk") that surrounds our featured strategy/standard focus. This *I Do* time goes by many titles in classrooms—model lesson, anchor lesson (Harvey and Goudvis 2000, 2007), mini-lesson, think-aloud—but, whatever you choose to call it, the premise remains the same. Our goal for our students is to make visible those unseen, internal processes of creating meaning from text so that students can take on these essential strategies and, in turn, become fluent in the meaning-making processes of a skilled reader (Marzano 2007).

A strong, modeled lesson begins with the teacher introducing the strategy focus for the lesson and "metacognizing," or thinking aloud about how to use that strategy during reading (or any new literacy learning). During the *I Do* phase of gradual release, the teacher controls the reading and highlights the featured strategic process, explaining what it is, why it is used, and how and when to use it. The teacher breaks down the strategy by defining its critical attributes and explains it in appropriate student language, step by step, so that students can observe the strategy incorporated into an authentic meaning-making context (Pearson and Gallagher 1983; Jensen 2000). The teacher then begins to engage the students in academic conversations centered on the strategy in action. Concrete demonstrations and examples of the implemented strategy set the stage for the shared, interactive practice to follow.

Here is a glimpse of modeled strategy use—*I Do*—excerpted from *You Can't Just Say It Louder! Differentiated Strategies for Comprehending Nonfiction.* (Murphy 2010, 109–112). Murphy selects the high-interest text "Cell Phone Agreement" for the seventh grade model lesson. She focuses on word-meaning strategies that incorporate some of the goals found in CCSS Reading Anchor Standard 4 and Language Anchor Standards 4–6. She demonstrates how good readers use both morphological and contextual "proof," when provided in the text, to figure out the meaning of unknown words using a novel process she calls Word Magician.

Figure 6.3 "Word Magician" Example

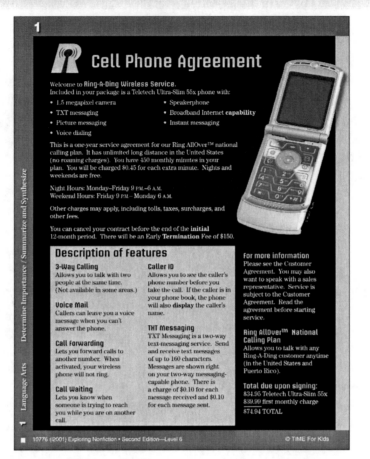

Good readers sometimes come to a word in a text and do not know its meaning. Just skipping words and reading on without solving the meaning of those unknown words can quickly get a reader confused about the big ideas of the text. Today, I am going to teach you a strategy called "Word Magician" that can help you figure out the meaning of an unknown, tricky word.

The first thing that a good word magician does is look *in* a word (see Figure 6.4). Look at the word that I am writing in the first column on our chart—*contract.* Let's look in this word to find a chunk or part we know—a root. The first chunk or root I recognize is *con-.* We have talked about the meaning of this prefix before. It means "with, together." I think that knowing this chunk will help me understand the meaning of *contract.*

There is another root of this word that I have heard before—*tract*. I need to think. What does *tract* mean? If I am not really sure what a word chunk means, it will not help me. However, I think I do know this Latin root. It means "pull" or "drag." Now, if I put these two parts together, the word *contract* may mean something that you pull together. I will write down my thinking in the second column.

Figure 6.4 "Word Magician Chart"—Look in the Word

The mystery word	What I see when I "look in" the word	What I see when I "look around" the word	What I think the word means
contract	*con* = with, together *tract* = pull, drag		

The next thing that a good word magician does is look *around* the word in the text for any clues or proof that will help me add to my thinking about what *contract* means. I will reread any text chunks that talk about this contract. I am looking for words or short phrases that point to the meaning of the word *contract*. I am going to underline those clues when I find them. The title is *Cell Phone Agreement*. The whole text is about this agreement. An agreement is when two people or groups decide to do something together. That's like pulling together to do something. I am going to underline *Agreement* in the title.

In paragraph two, when I read the first sentence, I see the phrase *one-year service agreement*. Now I know that this particular agreement is between the person who wants a cell phone and the cell phone service company. This agreement is for one year. I will underline this phrase as another clue to the meaning of *contract*.

In the fifth paragraph, I can reread the sentence that the word *contract* is actually in, and I learn that you can cancel a contract. This contract is for a 12-month period, or a year. I will underline *cancel* and *initial 12-month period*. Let's write all our clues on the chart.

Figure 6.5 "Word Magician Chart"—Look Around the Word

The mystery word	What I see when I "look in" the word	What I see when I "look around" the word	What I think the word means
contract	*con* = with, together *tract* = pull, drag	*agreement, one-year service agreement, cancel, initial 12-month period*	

Now I need to write what I think *contract* means in the last column. If I think about what I learned from looking in and looking around this word, then I think I am ready to say what *contract* means. I think a contract is an agreement that pulls two people or groups together for a certain period of time. In this article, the cell phone plan purchaser makes a contract or agreement with the cell phone company to buy cell phone service. Now I can write what I think *contract* means in the last column.

Figure 6.6 "Word Magician Chart"—Predicted Word Meaning

The mystery word	What I see when I "look in" the word	What I see when I "look around" the word	What I think the word means
contract	*con* = with, together *tract* = pull, drag	*agreement, one-year service agreement, cancel, initial 12-month period*	*a one-year agreement with Ring-A-Ding Wireless Service to buy a cell phone calling plan*

Along with the think-aloud that teachers provide in a model lesson, visual models of the teacher's patterns of strategic processing provide powerful links to how students apply and eventually self-monitor the strategy within their own reading. Many teachers display these visual models on strategy or anchor charts (popularized by the work of Harvey and Goudvis 2000, 2007) as a concrete reference to support students as they build a plethora of strategic moves to integrate into their meaning-making, problem-solving reading tools. A key feature of a strategic thinking chart is to use the students' own language while designing a visual of the critical attributes of the strategy in action—describing how to apply the strategy and what questions to consider while using that process before, during, and/or after reading. These charts can include features such as numbered steps, student sketches, illustrations, symbols, graphic organizers/thinking maps, or text and student-generated examples. We provide two samples of strategy charts, "STAR (Strategic Thinker and Reader) Points", developed by students in conjunction with the teacher after model lessons (Murphy 2010). The first "STAR Points" chart features the "Word Magician" word-solving strategy constructed after the above model lesson using input from the seventh grade students. This "STAR Points" chart defines the critical attributes the students used to figure out the meaning of unknown words that are contextually (and possibly morphologically) supported.

Figure 6.7 "STAR Points" Chart for the "Word Magician" Strategy

"STAR Points"

Word Magician:

A During-Reading Strategy

1. Identify a tricky word you do not understand.

2. Look in the word for chunks or parts you know.

3. Look around the word for clues that point to what the word means.

4. Think about the word now. What do you know? What is the best meaning for the word in this text?

5. If necessary, use a word resource to look up the word or to learn more about the word.

This second example of a "STAR Points" chart, created with a third-grade class after a model lesson, focuses on using a "text walk" to preview the text features of an informational text to look for main ideas that may be presented in the text (CCSS Reading: Informational Text, Supporting Standards 2 and 5, Grades K–3).

Figure 6.8 "STAR Points Chart"—Taking a Text Walk to Preview a Text for Main Ideas Strategy

"STAR Points"

Taking a Text Walk to Preview a Text for Main Ideas:

A Before-Reading Strategy

1. "Walk" the text from top to bottom.

2. Look at each text feature.

3. Ask myself, "What do I know now?"

4. Ask myself, "What questions do I have?"

5. Ask myself, "What is this text mostly about?"

6. Create my hypothesis for the main idea of the text.

Understanding *We Do*—Shared Strategy

During *We Do*, although the teacher still leads the literacy work, he or she gradually begins to hand off control of the strategy to the students, inviting them to try out the actions of the process in a "risk-free" environment. The students flow in and out of the interactive experience as they begin to comprehend and take on the procedural processes of the featured strategic work. The work of the *We Do* phase of gradual release is highly collaborative. Through rich conversations, the teacher and students discuss the critical attributes of the strategy and enter into targeted, shared practice embedded in authentic experiences with text. This *We Do* time buzzes with activity and intentional talk, or what Maria Nichols calls *purposeful talk*. "Purposeful talk is focused, collaborative talk; it is a social process that requires students to actively engage with ideas, think out loud together, and work to a co-construction of those ideas." (Nichols 2009, 12).

Discussing and responding as a whole class, with a small group, or in a partnership, the students practice the task with teacher support to ensure that the students experience incremental steps of success. The teacher serves as mentor to the students, moving about between the students as they share their actions and think with each other in response to what they have been asked to try out or discuss. The teacher observes, assesses, prompts for or suggests purposeful action, questions, gives specific feedback, reteaches when necessary, and provides time for reflection. Adjustments made by the teacher during this time involve pacing, the increments of practice, the specificity of the language used, and the reading level of the text example. Because the teacher controls the scaffolding of *We Do*, the text used during shared, interactive practice can be grade-level, complex text since the teacher often supports the reading of the text during this time (Routman 2003).

So, how would our seventh grade model lesson centered on the Word Magician word solving strategy evolve into the *We Do* level of gradual teacher release of responsibility? Let's continue the lesson as it moves into that shared interactive practice level.

> *Discussing and responding as a whole class, with a small group, or in a partnership, the students practice the task with teacher support to ensure that the students experience incremental steps of success. The teacher serves as mentor to the students, moving about between the students as they share their actions and think with each other in response to what they have been asked to try out or discuss.*

Let's find another word that we can use our "Word Magician" strategy to determine its meaning. In the fifth paragraph of the Cell Phone Agreement, where we came across the word *contract*, there is another tricky word— *termination*.

- What is the first thing that good word magicians do? *(Look in the word for chunks or parts they know.)*

- What do you know? (Possible responses: *The suffix is* -tion, *which means "state of," so the word must mean "the state of or act of terminating." I have seen a movie about a Terminator; he stops all the bad stuff that happens. I have heard the part* term, *but I do not know what it means.)*

Well, the only part that we seem to know for sure is that *-tion* is a suffix that can mean "state of, characterized by." Let's write that in our chart. Maybe we will find out if a *Terminator* who stops or ends bad things is somehow related to the word *termination*. What is the next thing that good word magicians do? (*Look around the word for clues to what the word means.*)

- Does anyone see any clues or proof for what *termination* might mean? (Prompt students if they need support. Possible responses: *You have to pay money, or a fee, if you do it early. I think it has something to do with canceling or stopping the cell phone service contract. You have to pay a fee if you cancel the agreement before the end of the 12-month period.*)

- So, what clues should I write in the chart? (*cancel your contract, before the end, early, fee*)

- Let's look at the last column of our chart. What do you think I should write here to explain what the word means? When we looked in the word, we determined that *termination* has to do with the state of or act of terminating. In the article, the word *termination* is being used to describe a fee that the cell phone company charges if the cell phone user cancels or ends the contract early. Do we think *termination* is when someone or something stops, ends, or cancels something? Let's write the meaning of *termination* in our own words in the last column.

Let's try to figure out the meaning of one more word, using our "Word Magician" strategy. The word *national* is in two places in our text—the second paragraph and in the heading Ring AllOver™ National Calling Plan. With your partner, use the "Word Magician" strategy to look in and look around the word and determine what you think the word means.

- Look at the word *national.* With your partner, discuss the first thing that a word magician does to figure out the meaning of a word. What do you see when you look in this word?

  Students often identify the chunk, nation, *in this word, but verify that they actually know what it means by asking, "What does nation mean?" Responses heard before include, "A nation ... is ... well, it's like ... a nation," and "A nation ... it's in our social studies book." These answers do not reflect a clear understanding of the concept behind the word and therefore do not help the reader.*

- What else does a good reader do to figure out the meaning of a word?

- With your partner, see what proof you can find for the meaning of the word *national.* (Possible responses*: second paragraph*—"in the United States"; *under the heading,* "Ring AllOver™ National Calling Plan"—"in the United States and Puerto Rico")

- Now work with your partner to decide on a meaning for the word *national* in this text. Be ready to share your thinking with the group.

While the *I Do* level of the gradual release of responsibility model is paramount for articulating and demonstrating the critical attributes and actions of a key strategy or standard for our students, the *We Do* shared, interactive level is an equally critical part of the "how" of delivering the CCSS to our students. Without this social learning and interactive practice between the teacher-expert and the students, the jump to the independent level of strategy use becomes a chasm for many students. Incomplete comprehension due to a lack of effective and successful practice time at the *We Do* level of support results in many students who only partially learn the new strategy with gaps in their procedural processing, ensuing in a habituation of errors during independent reading. Being right there as teacher and coach during this interactive practice, we can say, "This is what it looks like and sounds like. Go this way, not that way. Follow me!" Sufficient time spent together during *We Do* is never wasted. In fact, as students work out their confusions and firm up their understandings during this collaborative practice time, teachers discover that students require less time in small-group instructional practice before they are ready to take new learning to independence. We plan well for our shared, interactive practice because we really believe that for our students to achieve the "what" of the CCSS, they must have these supported "opportunities to talk about the hazy feelings, ideas, and images they have during reading. "Teachers need to provide plenty of time for [students] to talk about what they are thinking during reading. Through this talk, [students] can discover what they actually *do* think" (McGee 1995, 108).

Let's Think and Discuss

1. Think about your instruction or instruction that you have observed over the last week. How was shared, interactive practice incorporated before students were asked to take on the literacy work in a guided or independent context? What was the impact of the shared interactive practice on student achievement?

2. Select a Common Core State Standard that you are featuring in your instruction in the next few days. How will you model this standard for your students and demonstrate its use? How will you engage students in shared interactive practice with the standard in order to clear up any confusion the students might have or firm up their understanding of how the standard works in action?

Chapter 7

Moving into Small Instructional Groups: *You Try*—Guided Strategy Use

> *Guided instruction serves as a linchpin between the focused instruction students have received and the independent learning they will need to complete.*
> —Fisher and Frey 2014, 65

The third quadrant of the gradual release of responsibility model is the *You Try* or guided strategy use phase. "Teachers demonstrating or orchestrating high-level work do not necessarily achieve transference . . . ." Instruction must move "immediately from demonstrating reading skills to coaching students to do this work on their own and giving them feedback as they try it" (Calkins, Ehrenworth, and Lehman 2012, 68). Therefore, we strongly believe that this is a critical practice time in the instructional day for teachers to pull together small groups of students for reading—no more than six at a time—in a setting where every student in the group can be seen and heard. Too many students hide in the whole-group setting, becoming "invisible," unheard voices (Calkins, Erenworth, and Lehman 2012). At the end of the day, we do not really know what they were thinking, what they learned, or what they took on to employ independently as they read. No matter whether the student is a struggling, below-level reader or a quite proficient, above-level reader, all students need to be a part of a small reading or strategy group several times a week in which the text level, comprehension challenge, and opportunities for strategic problem solving are just right for them. It is during this time, meeting with just a few students, where we can truly tap into what strategies and CCSS our students have under control, note what they only partially know, and make informed decisions on what they need to take on next in their reading work. In this focused, guided context, real acceleration of student reading expertise can take place.

At the *You Try* phase, the students own the responsibility of working strategically through the text. The students read the selected text while making individual problem-solving decisions as they negotiate that text. During a small instructional group session, the teacher selects a specific focus to target (think CCSS) based on what the particular students need to practice or firm up while ensuring that the students engage with just-right, challenging text. According to Burkins and Croft, what is practiced in this context is not "novel" but provides "an indispensable area for linking skills and strategies that you have already taught, modeled, and practiced together during read-aloud, shared reading, and even individual conferences" (2010, 16). Most of the teacher talk from the modeled and shared/interactive levels of the gradual release model gives way to student self-talk and lively group discussions about text meaning, strategy work, and clarification of reading confusion. The questions we constantly keep in mind during this time are, *Who is doing the work? Who is being active in this reading process?* In this context, the response should be, the *students*!

Although the teacher turns over the reading to the students, he or she is right there with the group to monitor for student strengths and any ineffective student reading moves. This careful observation helps the teacher highlight effective student processing or prevent students' habituation of procedural-processing or strategic errors during the guided practice time before independence. The teacher "drops in" on students as they are reading to check for understanding, prompt and cue, clear up any confusion, redirect student intentions (reteaching, if needed), and provide specific feedback to students about what they did well or still need to work on as they read. During this time, the teacher expects to see student approximations and errors, but he or she is especially interested in what students do to monitor their own meaning making. The teacher notes the different "fix-up" strategies the students attempt in order to reestablish understanding. While the students incorporate practice of the featured teaching focus in that session's reading, the teacher also praises and/or prompts for the weaving together of all of the students' known monitoring and comprehension strategies as they read (Murphy 2010). Basically, the teacher coaches the students, bolstering them for independence and automaticity using their current repertoire of strategies. If students are not comfortably using these strategies/standards during the guided practice time, it is highly unlikely that we will see these behaviors during their independent reading or close reading experiences.

What is important to consider when designing this *You Try* time with your students? One question we ponder is: Who will be a part of this instructional reading group? These groups are flexible and dynamic, and the membership changes constantly based on feedback from our observations, formative assessments, and purpose or focus. We often select a group of students who read at a similar level of text difficulty. What does that mean in a Common Core world? From our chapter on text complexity, we have really expanded our thinking about text levels to include dimensions that are quantitative, qualitative, and reader/task oriented. When reflecting on the membership of a small instructional reading group, however, the teacher must ensure that all of the students in the group have text that they can read with just a few decoding challenges so that the students are freed up to focus on meaning (Allington 2012). Marie Clay reflects that students need "practice in orchestrating complex processing on just-difficult-enough texts" and, thus, over time, teachers can effectively move students "up a gradient of difficulty of texts which can support fluent and successful reading" (1993, 53). Burkins and Croft stress that when reading instructional text, "the text rather than the teacher should support the students as they develop a self-extending system" (2010, 50). The *You Try* level of the gradual release model is just one step away from independence, so while we attempt to keep the text complexity and the teaching focus at the cusp of the students' challenge level, we must also ensure that this setting is truly a practice time for students to develop flexibility and confidence in the strategies that they are bringing forward from the modeled, anchor lessons (*I Do*) and the ensuing shared/interactive practice (*We Do*).

Sometimes, teachers also create small instructional reading groups called strategy groups. Strategy groups are formed after modeled lessons with explicit demonstrations of a strategy and active, shared engagement with that particular strategy/standard. When the students move into independent practice, reading self-selected text to personally apply the strategy or standard, the teacher assembles different small instructional strategy groups for guided practice. Membership in a strategy group is temporary and may consist of students reading at multiple levels of text complexity. The students in the group bring their independent reading texts with them and decide with the teacher which text would provide a good try-out of the featured strategy. Each student in the group will most probably be reading a different text. (Keep in mind that any student-selected text must be on the independent level for that reader.) The students read and work on their own as the teacher "drops in" on every reader, discusses the meaning of a portion of the text, reflects with the student about his or her problem solving through the strategy work, and provides specific feedback or coaches the student, offering support only as needed. Students vary in the amount of scaffolding they may need. Some may just need to touch base to make sure that they are on the right track to become proficient with the strategy. Other students may need more demonstration, shared practice, or examples before they will own the strategy.

Close reading, model/anchor lessons, shared/interactive reading, and independent reading are essential components of a strong literacy learning continuum, but without small instructional reading groups, students lose essential guided practice time and teachers do not have access to these powerful, up-close assessment opportunities that inform instruction. Finding the time to meet with these small instructional reading or strategy groups is critical; therefore, the teacher establishes clear classroom routines at the beginning of the year and introduces powerful independent literacy engagements for students who are not currently working in a small group. There are multiple instructional configurations that teachers utilize for their literacy/ELA time, such as the Daily Five (Boushey and Moser 2006), literacy centers or stations, or reading workshops. All of these options, as well as others, when managed effectively, create an opportunity for teachers to pull small instructional reading/strategy groups while ensuring that the rest of the students participate in authentic, independent literacy activities.

> *Close reading, model/anchor lessons, shared/interactive reading, and independent reading are essential components of a strong literacy learning continuum, but without small instructional reading groups, students lose essential guided practice time, and teachers do not have access to these powerful, up-close assessment opportunities that inform instruction.*

So, how might a teacher go about planning a small group instructional reading group? What factors are important to consider in designing an effective roadmap for the lesson? Teachers need to carefully think through this time with students to provide targeted guided practice that will accelerate students into ownership of the strategies/standards in their independent reading. Below are suggested steps in developing a powerful plan for the *You Try* time with students.

1. **Consider**—Where are these students as readers? What strategies/processes do they have under control? What do they partially know or use as they read and need to practice in order to become skilled? Where do they need to go next as readers? (Decisions stem from ongoing assessment of where students are in their literacy processing.)

2. **Focus**—Set a focus for reading based on what these readers can do now and what they need to do next. Be prepared to succinctly state the focus for the students in the introduction to the reading for the day. Break down the strategy work or standard into its critical attributes, and know the student language that you will use to explicitly describe the lesson's focus.

3. **Select**—Match a just-right text to these readers. Consider all the factors of text complexity and how this text integrates with the teaching focus by providing opportunities for problem solving.

4. **Introduce**—Scaffold the students into the text through a conversation about that text. Keep frontloading of the text to a minimum. If necessary, provide essential support to address a unique challenge or share critical background knowledge that the students must have to enter the text with maximum meaning. Include the focus for reading stated in appropriate student language in the introduction.

5. **Read**—Ask the students to read the text or text chunk individually. Monitor, prompt, and observe or reinforce students' strategic actions such as word solving, searching and adjusting, self-correcting, maintaining fluency, and construction of meaning, especially noting how each student integrates the focus/goal into their reading processing.

6. **Discuss**—Listen to what the students say about the text and their reading work, and note how they demonstrate and control their level of understanding. Stopping the reading to have a conversation about the text may occur several times during the session.

7. **Revisit**—Return to the teaching focus with the students. Ask students to provide specific examples of how they used the strategy/standard in their reading. The teacher may illustrate the focus with student examples or provide a brief demonstration to revisit the strategy if necessary.

8. **Reflect**—Based on observation of students' problem solving as they read, consider if the featured strategy/standard should be a continued focus for small group instructional guided practice or decide if the students are ready to extend the strategy into personal practice through their independent reading.

During small instructional reading groups, the goal is the development of the effective strategic actions required for reading and comprehending text. Therefore, a clear focus drives the small group time and precedes even text selection as the first thing teachers consider when planning for this context. This focus is driven by assessment considerations: what you currently know about what your students can do as readers and the identification of what they need to take on next and firm up as evolving meaning makers during reading. Fountas and Pinnell identify three categories of strategic thinking—thinking within the text, thinking beyond the text, and thinking about the text (2010). Significant reading strategies (and the CCSS) fall into these categories. Thinking within the text includes such strategies as word solving, monitoring and adjusting, searching for and responding to text cues and information, fluency, and summarizing. Note that the CCSS Foundational Skills Anchor Standards and the Language Anchor Standards fall into thinking within the text. Predicting, inferring, and creating/synthesizing require readers to think beyond the text. Analyzing and critiquing/evaluating happen when the reader really thinks about the text. Thinking beyond the text and thinking about the text engages students in the higher-order thinking required by the CCSS. Remember that honing in on a focus for a particular small instructional reading group does not mean that students' known strategies are not called into play during the session. It just means that as readers, the students particularly attend to the featured strategy or standard and actively engage in practice with you as the guide or coach on the sidelines.

We will illustrate a possible planning sequence for working with a small instructional reading group with an example from our own experience. It is important to state that this example is a way to plan for a small instructional group using this particular text; it is not *the* way. Small group instructional plans are flexible based on what level the group members are at currently as readers. Your assessment of what the students need in order to demonstrate fluent, automatic strategic processing drives the focus and text you select. Small group guided instructional groups have many faces (literally and figuratively), and the lessons may reflect multiple formats depending on a variety of factors. This particular small group consists of five second graders who are reading grade-level texts. They have strong foundational skills, and they are able to decode developmentally appropriate multisyllable words. They quickly respond to literal level questions and locate textual proof for their responses, and they are engaging in increasingly complex inferential thinking. These students are working on self-monitoring text meaning by searching for and integrating multiple cue sources. The students have had limited exposure to informational text during reading, so they have recently participated in several different model lessons and shared/interactive practice sessions using informational text (driven by the grade-level CCSS for this type of text). These engagements centered on previewing text features to help identify the main idea(s) and the purpose/structure of a text before reading as well as using the language of the text to visualize critical text details. We also note that these students have never encountered a procedural text in their reading. Therefore, we set the following focus for the small group practice: Students *use text features to locate key facts and information* as well as to *identify the main topic/text structure/purpose*. Then, students visualize the content of the text as they read to *describe the connections between the steps in procedures in a text*. (Italicized words excerpted from the second grade CCSS Reading: Informational Text Standards.)

Note that this is a challenging focus for second grade students—one that nudges them to independence using these standards. This instructional focus identifies strategies that the students have seen modeled/demonstrated and then practiced interactively with teacher-scaffolded support. The students are now ready for a release of responsibility as they attempt to personally take on the strategic processing in a guided practice session with us. We are ready to observe and check for understanding to see who is beginning to take ownership of this reading work as well as note how effectively the students process this less familiar text structure using the strategies they have learned. Perusing the Informational Text standards for second grade, we also see that we may observe other strategies in play during the reading, although those standards are not the stated focus of the small group session. For example, one Language Standard for second grade states, *"Determine the meaning of words and phrases in a text . . ."* We always expect our students to attend to the vocabulary and utilize their known word strategies to figure out a new word if possible. We recognize the critical nature of understanding word meaning in order to be able to visualize the big ideas of this informational text.

Once we have selected a focus for a particular small instructional reading group, we match a just-right text to our readers and the highlighted strategy. We consider the complexity of the text to make sure that it is challenging yet accessible to the students. Decoding work is within their problem-solving scope, freeing them up to focus on meaning. Most of the time, multiple texts can serve as possible choices to provide students with practice using a featured strategy. However, some strategies take on a different dimension when encountered in another genre, and some CCSS change in nature between literary and informational standards. We recommend that at least half the texts that your students read and respond to in small instructional reading groups are informational texts so that students have many opportunities to use their strategic processing and the CCSS Informational Anchor Standards during guided practice. Content-area teachers can also use the small instructional reading group format with subject-specific text to offer students practice in reading texts where they will encounter such things as new content-area vocabulary and knowledge, a variety of text structures and text features, and frequent opportunities to support their thinking with text evidence.

Now we select an appropriate text for this group of students. Since we want to choose a procedural text that is at a just-right challenge level, we find the text titled "Pick-a-Coin Game" in Figure 7.1 (*Exploring Nonfiction: A Differentiated Content-Area Reading Program, Second Grade*). (See Figure 7.1)

This text is, quantitatively speaking, a good text level for these students, and the fact that it describes how to play a game should be interesting to our readers, especially since most of them have played a game with rules. The text features support the topic, structure, and purpose, and the text offers our students a chance to apply the focus. The numbered steps within the text provide a nice introduction for these students to one possible feature of procedural text. Because the focus centers on the importance of text features and "making mind pictures" (visualizing) to construct meaning, we plan to have the students add some of their own text features to the text as they read by drawing simple sketches to accompany the steps in a process—the directions. These sketches will help us know how successfully the students comprehend the text. Finally, as we look at this text, we like the connection of the topic to math since these students are also working with money concepts.

Figure 7.1 Pick-a-Coin Game

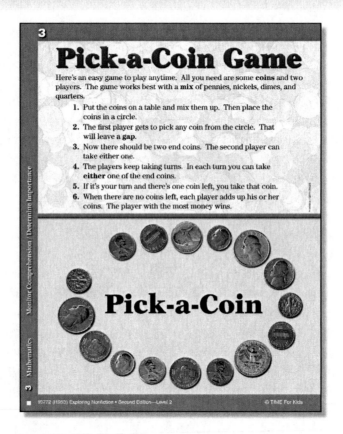

So what have we completed so far in the planning process for our small instructional reading group?

1. **Consider**—Where are these students as readers? What strategies/ processes do they have under control? What do they partially know or use as they read, and what do they need to practice in order to become skilled? Where do they need to go next as readers? (Decisions stem from ongoing assessment of where students are in their literacy processing.)

2. **Focus**—Set a focus for reading based on what these readers can do now and what they need to do next. Be prepared to succinctly state the focus for the students in the introduction to the reading for the day. Break down the strategy work or standard into its critical attributes, and know the student language that you will use to explicitly describe the lesson's focus.

3. **Select**—Match a just-right text to these readers. Consider all the factors of text complexity and how this text integrates with the teaching focus by providing opportunities for problem solving.

What's next as we map out our time with this small instructional group?

4. **Introduce**—Scaffold the students into the text through a conversation about that text. Keep frontloading of the text to a minimum. If necessary, provide essential support to address a unique challenge or share critical background knowledge that the students must have to enter the text with maximum meaning. Include the focus for reading stated in appropriate student language as a part of the introduction.

At this point in our planning, we consider what we need to do before reading to set the students up for success. We know at the end of the text introduction that we always state the focus for the lesson for the students and remind them to use that strategy/standard as they read. In a strategy instructional group, setting the stage for the strategy/standard focus is all we would do to get the students ready for reading as they bring their own independent-level texts to the group context. But what about providing an actual introduction to the text when the students are going to read the same text in a small guided practice group? We consider that when students read independently, one goal for them is that they use the text and its features to select a text and prepare themselves for digging into that new text. Therefore, when planning an introduction for an instructional group text, we only provide essential support, turning the majority of the previewing or meaning-making before reading over to the students. The introduction is a brief, interactive conversation about the text, and the teacher does not reveal everything about the text or do the reading work for the students. As a result, text introductions vary greatly since texts change along with the multiple experiences and understandings that students bring to the reading table. Remember, we are working toward letting the text be the "teacher," so the students uncover the layers of meaning on their own.

When pulling together our thoughts about an introduction, we like to ask ourselves the question, *What do the students need to know to access the meaning of this text?* This question allows broad consideration of possible reader challenges such as "tricky" words—in decoding or uncovering a word's meaning, text genre and/or structure, or any background knowledge critical to understand the text. If there are too many challenges to address in an introduction, then likely the text selected is not in the instructional range for the students and will prove to be a frustrating read where the teacher finds that he or she is doing all the work to maneuver the students through the text. In our "Pick-a-Coin Game" text, there is minimal, if any, significant decoding work that would offer the students a problem. Some possible unknown vocabulary includes *coin, mix* (used both as a noun and a verb in the text), *gap, either,* and *turn* (as a multiple meaning word). However, we decide that since the students are going to read the text in meaningful chunks, stopping to talk after each section, we will deal with the vocabulary—with the exception of the word *coin*—during the text reading. At each "stop and think" spot, the students establish the meaning of any key vocabulary in order to visualize the game's directions and sketch a text feature. The biggest challenge before reading is the text structure, as we know that these students have not yet encountered a procedural text in their own reading. However, since we are holding the students accountable for practicing a preview of the text features to determine main ideas, text structure, and purpose rather than a teacher-directed introduction, we plan to let the students lead the way in setting themselves up to read through a collaborative conversation before reading.

Teacher:	*Here is our text for today.*
Student:	*Oh! Money!*
Student:	*Pick-a-Coin Game. Oh, yeah! We are going to read about a game. I love games.*
Teacher:	*So, what should we do first?*
Student:	*We need to look at all the text features so we will know the big ideas before we read. And also, we can maybe figure out the author's purpose for writing this.*
Student	*I know his purpose! He wants to teach us a game!*
Teacher:	*What text feature will you look at first?*

Student: Well, we read the title. It's in big red letters, so it's important.

Student: I think it also probably tells us that it's going to be about a game.

Student: Yeah. And I see numbers in the writing part. Why are they there?

Student: Well, maybe it's a list of what you need.

Student: No, there's too much writing after each number.

Student: I know! I bet it's like—you know—directions. Like do number one first, number two second, number three next. You know, like that!

Student: I know that's how games work.

Teacher: So you think that the numbers are the steps to playing the Pick-a-Coin game, and if we read and do each of the directions in order, we can play the game?

Student: Yes! There are six steps. I wonder if it will be a hard game to play? I can't wait to try! Can we play it after we read? Please?

Teacher: Of course! Are there any other text features that we should look at?

Student: There are some bold words. They must be important—coins, mix, gap, and, hmmm . . .

Student: I know that one. It's either.

Student: And there is a photo of a bunch of money with the name of the game in the middle. You must need money to play this game.

Student: I see pennies and dimes and nickels and quarters. They're in a circle.

Teacher: So I have a question. This is called Pick-a-Coin Game, but what is a coin?

Student: I don't know.

Student: Me either!

Teacher: Do you think that there is anything in a text feature that might help you figure out the meaning of the word coin? I think it must be important for us to know since it is in the name of the game.

Student: Oh, wait. I think I know. Look at the picture. I think that all that money is like coins. So when it is your turn, you get to pick one. Yeah, coin is money like a penny or a nickel.

Teacher:	When we read, we will see if you are right. So you think that this text is about how to play the Pick-a-Coin game?
Student:	Yes, and you get to find out the directions so you can play it.
Teacher:	This is a special kind of text that tells the reader how to do something; in this case, it will tell us the steps of how to play a game. When you looked at the text features, you figured out what you think is the main idea of the text, the author's purpose for writing the text, and how the text is written. Good readers carefully look at the text features in informational text before reading so they will be ready to read with understanding.
Student:	We're getting good at this.
Teacher:	Yes, you are really using the text features to give you clues about what you will read.
Student:	I looked in the text features in my shark book yesterday to know what the page would be about.
Student:	You're smart to do that!
Teacher:	Now we will read the text a chunk at a time. Then we will stop and check to make sure that we really understand that part of the text. We will try to picture each step of the directions in our mind to make sure that we can play the game correctly when we finish. As we visualize each step, I thought that we could make a quick sketch of our "mind picture" to go with that step so we can make sure that we know exactly what to do when we play the game. We can create our own text feature for each step. Sketching our "mind pictures" is one thing that good readers can do to monitor their understanding. Finally, we will use the text and our own text features to help us play the game.
Student:	I wonder why the author didn't put pictures for each direction. But now, I can look at my own text features to win the game!
Student:	We visualized our reading and sketched in science last week. You showed us how. We are good at visualizing, aren't we?
Teacher:	The best! What do you think should be our first reading "think stop"?
Student:	I think we should read until we get to step number one. Okay?

You can see from the above text introduction that the students are active in building meaning before they read. They are moving toward independence with the standards represented in the teaching focus. We have an authentic conversation with the students about the text and offer just a few prompts or questions to keep the students on track. We also quickly summarize their processing of what they learned from the text features; and then, we end by presenting the focus for the reading today. The students actually set their own purpose for reading—they want to play the game! Remember, the students are reaching toward independence with these strategies because they have participated in significant shared/interactive practice following teacher-modeled demonstrations and examples.

Now, the students are ready to jump into the text.

5. **Read**—Ask the students to read the text or text chunk individually. Monitor, prompt, and observe or reinforce students' strategic actions such as word solving, searching and adjusting, self-correcting, maintaining fluency, and construction of meaning, especially noting how each student integrates the focus/goal into his or her reading processing.

6. **Discuss**—Listen to what the students say about the text and their reading work, and note how they demonstrate and control their level of understanding. Stopping the reading to have a conversation about the text may occur several times during the session.

The teacher establishes clear routines in the small instructional reading group time that require the students to take control of and do the reading work of processing the text and constructing meaning. The students read silently and simultaneously. Round-robin reading in which students take turns reading the text aloud is not appropriate during this time (Allington and Rasinski 1998). Every student needs to be fully engaged in reading 100 percent of the text. Even less-experienced readers read a carefully selected text at their reading level on their own, although they may "whisper-read" (subvocalize) quietly as they read. These students move into silent reading as soon as they are ready, usually by the end-of-first-grade text levels. Early levels of texts are short in length and can be read and discussed in their entirety during the guided practice time, while older students reading longer texts may focus on only a few pages or chunks of text during a small group session. The teacher and students may stop at several points during the reading to discuss the text, ask and respond to questions, or note how they used a strategy to problem-solve.

The teacher's primary role during the text reading is to drop in on individual students after they silently read a portion of the text and listen to what they say about the text, noting how they demonstrate their level of understanding. With early readers, the teacher may ask a student to softly read aloud a part of the text in order to monitor that student's word processing and strategic problem-solving. While moving around to interact with all the students in the group, the teacher checks for comprehension; gives the students the opportunity to share their questions, thoughts, or possible confusions; and monitors how the students are using the teaching focus. The art of scaffolding comes into play as the students read and respond to the text. Different students will encounter different challenges. Hopefully, students will dip into a plethora of problem solving strategies in order to get back on track after they get "stuck." Frequently, the teacher observes and specifically praises what the student just effectively demonstrated as a reader to reinforce that problem-solving strategy for future use. Sometimes, the teacher may only ask a quick question or offer a simple prompt to help a student solve a tricky part, but occasionally, the teacher may have to intervene with more support, such as a quick demonstration or a reteach of a strategic move. As the students read, the teacher jots down brief notes to document the students' actions or responses and to look for quick teaching points to reinforce.

In the case of our model lesson with the "Pick-a-Coin Game" text, the students silently read the text in seven chunks—the introduction and the six steps, stopping after each part to discuss what was read and visualize what they need to do to play the game. After silently reading the first chunk—the introductory paragraph—the students find text proof to ascertain that the word *coins* does indeed refer to the pennies, nickels, dimes, and quarters—the materials needed to play the game. They also discuss the meaning of *mix*, using the picture clue to help them. The students agree that they would label this section *What You Need* (to play the game).

Next, the students fold a 12 x 18-inch sheet of white construction paper into six boxes and number each box in the upper left-hand corner to represent the six steps of the directions to play the game. After they read each direction or step in the text, the students stop to discuss the meaning. Then they quickly sketch what they are supposed to do in that step of the game. Sometimes the students ask if they can dramatize the step before they sketch it. We share our "mind pictures" each time and discuss which words or phrases help us capture the important details in that step. Step 2 provides a challenge as we have to figure out the meaning of *gap* as it is necessary to our understanding of what to do next. Several of the students point out the space in the circle of coins in the photograph (thank goodness for text features). As the students read, discuss, and sketch what they have visualized, we carefully monitor their meaning-making to see if they are ready to take these strategies into their independent reading.

At the close of the lesson, revisiting the students' reading work reinforces the teaching focus and other effective strategic moves by the students.

7. **Revisit**—Return to the teaching focus with the students. Ask students to provide specific examples of how they used the strategy/standard in their reading. The teacher may illustrate the focus with student examples or provide a brief demonstration to revisit the strategy if necessary.

8. **Reflect**—Based on observation of students' problem solving as they read, consider if the featured strategy/standard should be a continued focus for small group instructional guided practice or decide if the students are ready to extend the strategy into personal practice through their independent reading.

Once the students read and react to the text, the teacher closes the small group guided practice time by revisiting several places where the students successfully problem-solved as they read. This quick, specific feedback reinforces those effective strategic moves so that the students will use them again. To encourage the students to take ownership of the instructional focus, they share examples of how they used the featured strategy/standard, solved their confusions, and orchestrated their strategies as they read. Remind the students to extend what they practiced today into their independent reading. Of course, the students cannot wait to play the game with a partner several times to check their own understanding of the procedures and develop a winning strategy. Then the group is off to teach the game to the rest of the class! (We note that the students refer to the text and their sketched text features several times as they play the game.)

If some of the students struggle a little with the teaching focus, decide if you need to reteach the focus objective or provide another experience with the strategy/standard. Ask yourself these questions: *Do I need to try a different text with this group in the next day or so using this same teaching focus? Do some of these students need more modeling and explanation or shared practice?* Perhaps several of the students encountered reading challenges apart from the day's focus.

Consider what those students need to know next. What should be the next featured strategy or standard for them? Should the instruction be at the *You Try* level, or do you need to dip back into a more supportive role such as in the *We Do* or even, *I Do* stage?

A teacher's reflection after the lesson drives future instruction and ensures that the teacher keeps students working at the cusp of their challenge level. Careful monitoring helps the teacher know when to move students up the ladder of text complexity. Time spent with small groups of students puts teachers up close to firm up powerful reading strategies, clarify confusions, and recognize when to nudge students into increasing independence. Small-group reading instruction provides the practice arena to accelerate learning.

We are intentional in our planning process and always record our thinking when designing a session with a small reading group. Some teachers are required to turn in their ELA/reading lesson plans to their principal each week, complete with the CCSS addressed in each lesson, while some teachers just jot their planning thoughts on sticky notes, which are then placed at appropriate places within the teacher's copy of the selected text as reminders of how the teacher intends to interact throughout the reading. No matter the format of your planning, powerful small group reading instruction results

A teacher's reflection after the lesson drives future instruction and ensures that the teacher keeps students working at the cusp of their challenge level. Careful monitoring helps the teacher know when to move students up the ladder of text complexity. Time spent with small groups of students puts teachers up close to firm up powerful reading strategies, clarify confusions, and recognize when to nudge students into increasing independence. Small-group reading instruction provides the practice arena to accelerate learning.

from thoughtful reflection on how to fully engage students in active targeted reading practice that meets the expectations of the CCSS for your grade level. Below is one choice of a template that we like to use to formulate our plans for small instructional reading groups.

Figure 7.2 Example Planning Tool Template for Small Instructional Reading Groups

Group Members:	
Text Selection:	
Teaching Focus What is the known featured standard/strategy that the students are accountable for practicing during their reading? *(Several CCSS/strategies may be integrated during the text reading.)*	
Background Knowledge/Vocabulary What are the supports for students in background knowledge or vocabulary? What do they already know? What might be a challenge in background knowledge or vocabulary for the students?	
Text Introduction How will I engage the students in a conversation about text before reading? Is there any critical background knowledge and/or a unique challenge that must be addressed before reading for the students to access the meaning of the text? (Remember to keep frontloading of the text to a minimum.) Have I named the teaching focus for the students and reminded them to use it during their reading?	
Text Reading and Discussion What is my plan for the text reading? At what points in the text will the students stop and think/discuss? What questions can be posed to students as they read?	
Revisit the Reading What did students do well? What teaching points need to be made? How can I link students back to the teaching focus?	
Reflections Based on my observations, what is my next instructional move with these students?	

Here is an example of this planning tool for the second grade group reading the text the Pick-a-Coin Game. You may not fill out your plan with as much detail after you get used to the lesson sequence. Certainly, as you construct your lesson with this template, you could use short bullets and phrases to denote your main points and intended interactions, as this is your personal guide to reference as you teach.

Figure 7.3 Example Planning Tool for Second Grade Instructional Reading Group

Group Members:	
Text Selection: "Pick-a-Coin Game" (Second grade on-level text)	
Teaching Focus What is the known featured standard/strategy that the students are accountable for practicing during their reading? (Several standards/strategies may be integrated during the text reading.)	(Note: italicized text is from CCSS) Students *use text features to locate key facts and information* as well as to *identify the main topic/text structure/purpose.* Then, students visualize the content of the text as they read to *describe the connections between the steps in procedures in a text.*
Background Knowledge/Vocabulary What are the supports for students in background knowledge or vocabulary? What do they already know? What might be a challenge in background knowledge or vocabulary for the students?	**Background Knowledge—Support:** Students probably played a game with rules; exposure to the name and values of coins (from math lessons); **Challenge:** procedural text structure with steps in a process **Vocabulary**—*coins, mix* (as a noun and a verb), *gap, either, turn* (as a multiple meaning word)—do not frontload but wait until students encounter vocabulary in text; they use context/text features to word solve

Text Introduction How will I engage the students in a conversation about the text before reading? Is there any critical background knowledge and/or a unique challenge that must be addressed before reading for the students to access the meaning of the text? (Remember to keep "frontloading" of the text to a minimum.) Have I named the teaching focus for the students and reminded them to use it during their reading?	Preview the text with a student-led text walk—title, bold words, numbers, photograph. If necessary, ask: *What do you notice about how this text is set up? Why do you think there are numbers? What does the photograph tell us about the game? What do you think is the main idea of this text? What is the author's purpose?* Say: "You have already done one strategy that good readers do when reading text—you previewed the text features to find out the main idea and the author's purpose. We also know that it is a text that has directions or steps that we need to do in the right order so we can play the game." "Now, as we read the text, we need to visualize or picture the directions in our minds to make sure that we can play the game correctly when we are finished reading. We will sketch our mind pictures as we visualize to help understand and remember the most important details."
Text Reading and Discussion What is my plan for the text reading? At what points in the text will the students stop and think/discuss? What questions could be posed to students as they read?	Students fold an 11-by-18 inch sheet of white construction paper and number the boxes 1–6. Students stop after reading each direction to discuss what they are supposed to do. Then they sketch their "mind picture" of that step quickly in the appropriate box to create their own text feature. **Potential Questions:** What clues does the author give to help you understand the meaning of *coins*? How does the photograph help you figure out the meaning of *gap*? Why did the author include the numbered steps? How does that help you play the game? What would happen if you did not follow the directions in order? Did visualizing and sketching your own text feature help you better understand the text? How?
Revisit the Reading What did students do well? What teaching points need to be made? How can I link students back to the teaching focus?	(*Record as students read, process, and discuss text.*)
Reflections Based on my observations, what is my next instructional move with these students?	(*Jot down after lesson.*)

Small instructional reading groups for emergent readers reflect many of the same characteristics as our second grade example. Since kindergartners and first graders are learning to decode text and working on multiple foundational skills, the teaching focus often combines several CCSS. However, we want all of these early readers to not only read the words but also construct meaning as they read. Susan Hill describes these two student reading roles as "code breaker" and "meaning maker" (1999). The following plan for a kindergarten instructional reading group encompasses both roles by including standards from the Foundational Anchor Standards and the Reading Standards in the teaching focus. This particular kindergarten group is integrating three foundational anchor standards into their reading. Note that for the lesson, these standards are framed for the students in the language they are using to name, describe, and practice these strategies. Several teacher prompts for these standards as the students are currently applying them follow in parentheticals after each standard.

Understand that words are separated by spaces in print. (Can you make it match? *[Text word to spoken word read]*)

Demonstrate basic knowledge of one-to-one letter-sound correspondences by producing the primary sound or many of the most frequent sounds for each consonant. (What do you see at the beginning of the word? Get your mouth ready. Does it look right?)

Read common high-frequency words by sight (e.g., *the, of, to, you, she, my, is, are, do, does*). (Can you frame and read the word, _____ ? *[Students use their two index fingers to frame the word in the text.]* This word is on our word wall.)

The teacher is also scaffolding support to help students develop these "meaning-making" kindergarten Reading Standards:

With prompting and support, describe the relationship between illustrations and the text in which they appear (e.g., what person, place, thing, or idea in the text an illustration depicts). (Check the picture/photograph/text feature. Does what you read make sense?)

With prompting and support, identify the main topic and retell key details of a text. (What is this mostly about?)

The students who participate in the following lesson example are becoming fairly proficient with one-to-one matching of the spoken word to the written word as they read. They have had many shared/interactive practice opportunities to use the pictures or text features to check meaning and get a new word started by considering their known initial visual information. As readers, they are practicing two ways of reading an unknown word by cross-checking the meaning gained from the supportive illustration with the beginning sound of the word by getting their mouth ready to say the word. (Clay 1991; Fountas and Pinnell 1996). These students also have "tried on" the comprehension focus of finding the main idea during many read-aloud and shared reading experiences. Now the teacher creates this small instructional group lesson plan designed to scaffold the reading work of the book *Places to Go*, over to the students— both the decoding and the comprehension. See Appendix A Teacher Resources for the complete text of *Places to Go*, TIME for Kids Nonfiction Readers.

Figure 7.4 Example Planning Tool for *Places to Go, TIME for Kids Nonfiction Readers*

Group Members:	
Text Selection: *Places to Go, TIME for Kids Nonfiction Readers,* TCM, 2012 (Emergent Level)	
Teaching Focus What is the known featured standard/strategy that the students are accountable for practicing during their reading? (Several standards/ strategies may be integrated during the text reading.)	Students maintain a one-to-one match of print across two lines of print. (ongoing) Students recognize and read the high-frequency word *you.* (ongoing) Students cross-check two cue sources when they read—meaning (photograph) and initial visual information. Students identify main idea ("mostly about") and several supporting details.

Background Knowledge/ Vocabulary What are the supports for students in background knowledge or vocabulary? What do they already know? What might be a challenge in background knowledge or vocabulary for the students?	**Background Knowledge—Support**: different places that students have gone; highly supportive photographs; **Challenge**: place where students may not have gone or do not know what it is called **Vocabulary**—location words—*farm, beach, mountain, forest, zoo, store*—do not frontload; leave for students to problem-solve by cross-checking, provide support during reading if student has tried several strategic moves first
Text Introduction How will I engage the students in a conversation about text before reading? Is there any critical background knowledge and/or a unique challenge that must be addressed before reading for the students to access the meaning of the text? (Remember to keep "frontloading" of the text to a minimum.) Have I named the teaching focus for the students and reminded them to use it during their reading?	You can go many places. What should we do before we read this informational book? (Prompt if necessary for students to take a text walk and have a conversation about the pictures of the places.) You have already done one strategy good readers do before reading a book (text walk). What do you think this book will be mostly about? (Students respond.) Good for you! I think that is the main idea of the book, too. When we read, we will find out the places that we can go. Those places will be the details that tell the names of the places. Be ready to name some of the places that you read about in the book. Today when you read, if you get stuck on a tricky part, what can you do to help yourself? Remember that we know three things now that we can do. (Look at the picture: Does it make sense? Get our mouth ready to start the "tricky word." Reread to see if it makes sense and looks right.)
Text Reading and Discussion What is my plan for the text reading? At what points in the text will the students stop and think/discuss? What questions could be posed to students as they read?	Read the first page together. Then students quietly and independently whisper-read the rest of the book. "Drop in" on readers to discuss their reading and strategy work. **Potential Questions:** This is a tricky part for you. What can you do to help yourself? What else can you try? Did that work for you? When you get finished reading, can you go back and find "proof" for at least four places that you can go?
Revisit the Reading What did students do well? What teaching points need to be made? How can I link students back to the teaching focus?	*(Record as students read, process, and discuss text. Provide specific examples of where students used cross-checking of two cue sources.)*

Reflections	(Jot down after lesson.)
Based on my observations, what is my next instructional move with these students?	Tomorrow, have students reread the book and create a part-to-whole thinking map with the main idea and the significant details—places. Ask the students to return to the text for proof, using both the pictures and the words in the text as their evidence.

When we consider small group instructional reading at the upper levels, we like what Donnelley and Donnelley (2012) have to say: "The teacher is an active member of the group and prompts students to think deeply about the text through targeted questioning . . . [the teacher] emphasizes more independent learning appropriate to the adolescent's reading needs. By listening to student responses . . . the middle school teacher can determine the need for follow-up mini-lessons . . . that will enable students to further probe the text. We have discovered that independent readers need to be monitored and guided just as carefully as those students who struggle with reading" (27). Students in the upper elementary grades and at the secondary level often read longer texts or text chunks/excerpts outside the actual instructional group's meeting time. The text selection provides a challenging yet achievable reading stretch for the students. Before reading, the teacher gathers a small group of students together to briefly set the stage for the featured text with a short introductory conversation, and then explicitly presents the focus or agenda for the day's reading. The teacher fosters a can-do spirit or a sense of urgency, reinforcing students to carry with them the current strengths required to be successful in the reading task (Serravallo 2010; Johnston 2004).

If necessary, before reading, the teacher scaffolds the students into the selected strategy/standard focus with a short refresher demonstration or explanation, and then gets the students started, using the teaching focus with their own text. As they leave the group, the students negotiate the amount of text to be read before they meet again to discuss their thinking about the text. The students independently read their own text and respond to that text per expectations, working at their own pace to prepare for the next set time the group meets to discuss what was read. Students choose from a repertoire of ways they can annotate their thinking as they read (sticky notes, margin notes, reading notebooks, etc.) so they can later share with the group any salient points, questions, thoughts, or confusions as well as be ready to support their ideas with textual evidence.

When the small group reconvenes, the teacher continues with the plan for the group. The teacher is integral to the meeting and helps guide the conversations about the text's meaning while probing for deeper understandings using higher-level questions. The teacher makes decisions based on students' responses to specifically affirm, prompt for further thought, or reteach if necessary. The teacher also has the option to refrain from commenting and become an observer as the students become more autonomous and participate in lively, thought-provoking conversations about the text. The teacher serves both as an active listener and a coach, bringing students back to the text to defend their opinions/arguments and debriefing strategic processing moves, especially those centered around the teaching focus. Finally, the teacher and students discuss how their current strategic work links to their independent reading both in ELA and the content areas. After the small-group meetings, the teacher reflects on what the students did well and where they need to go next in taking on the rigorous standards of the Common Core through engagement with increasingly complex text across multiple genres. This smaller group context, in which every member is active and accountable, is essential for building the reading expertise, depth of thinking, and confidence that students need to meet the challenge of the CCSS through a close reading of text.

We mentioned earlier in the chapter that small strategy instructional groups are an effective option to bring together several students who need practice on an identified strategy or specific standard. Once again, this is a strategy or standard that has been modeled and interactively practiced several times. Now the teacher, as coach on the side during a small strategy group, is ready to observe if the students effectively employ the featured focus in their own self-selected, independent text. As the group convenes, the teacher sets the agenda or purpose for the group and makes the decision as to whether or not these students need a quick demonstration or an example of expected strategic work before they engage in practice with their own reading. Since most of these students will likely bring a different text to the group meeting to try out the strategy/standard, we modify the planning template to reflect the change in the structure. See the example below:

Figure 7.5 Example Planning Tool for Small Instructional Strategy Group

Plan for Small Instructional Strategy Group	
Group Members:	
Teaching Focus What is the known featured standard/strategy that the students are accountable for practicing during their reading? (Several standards/strategies may be integrated during the text reading.) Do I need to provide a quick demonstration or example of the focus before the students begin their own reading?	Using textual evidence from their self-selected independent-level short story, students identify at least two character traits describing the main character at the beginning of the story. After reading, students identify at least two character traits describing the main character at the end of the story, describing any change in that character over the course of the story. The students defend their choices based on plot events or characters' dialogue. (Note: italicized text is from CCSS) *Analyze how particular lines of dialogue or incidents in a story or drama propel the action, reveal aspects of a character, or provoke a decision.*
Student: **Selected Text:**	**Observations/Comments/Teaching Points**
Student: **Selected Text:**	**Observations/Comments/Teaching Points**
Student: **Selected Text:**	**Observations/Comments/Teaching Points**

Student:	Observations/Comments/Teaching Points
Selected Text:	
Reflections Based on my observations, what is my next instructional move with these students?	*(Jot down after observations/interactions with each student)*

If you choose to structure your small instructional reading groups, the key factor is that you find the time to meet with these groups so that you can hear every student voice. The *You Try* setting allows us to check the "reading pulse" of our students and their ownership of significant strategies and standards. The critical data that we gather in these special, up-close encounters with our students becomes invaluable as we target our instructional craft and design guided practice times that are truly just what our students need to accelerate their progress. We wholeheartedly agree with Daniels and Harvey as we reflect on the power of small-group, collaborative conversations and the co-construction of meaning with our students: "In small groups, we are smarter. In well-structured groups, we leverage each other's thinking. We learn more not just because we all bring different pieces of the puzzle, but because, through talk, we can actually make new and better meaning together" (2009, 38).

Let's Think and Discuss

1. How can incorporating small groups allow you to effectively differentiate for your students' varying strengths and learning needs as they meet the challenge of the Common Core State Standards?

2. Think about the impact of using a purposeful design for small-group instruction, such as the one presented in the lesson plan template. How might using a plan like this help you organize your thinking before a lesson so that you can tighten your focus and maximize your time in a small group with your students?

Chapter 8

Independent Reading: *You Do*—Independent Strategy Use

> The gradual release of responsibility instructional framework is not something that can be implemented overnight, but it can be done sucessfully over time.
> —Fisher and Frey 2014, 145

Picture a classroom where students are intently reading both fiction and informational texts. Each student has a personal book bag or box filled with self-selected books, and students pore over them eagerly. The teacher visits with one student here, drops in on a small student-led text discussion, and does a quick informal assessment with another student while individual students read and respond to text or engage in hushed conversations about their reading selections. Although students are independently reading texts that are just right for them, this teacher maintains an active presence. When he or she is not working with a small instructional or strategy group, you may find this teacher chatting with a student about his text choice, checking for student clarity on an independent reading standards-based focus, dropping in to observe one student's strategic processing, conferencing with a student about reading goals, or challenging a student's thinking with a critical question about what he or she is reading. Yet this teacher knows that "scaffolding toward independence is not about teachers knowing how to hold the readers up; it is about knowing how to let the readers go" (Burkins and Croft 2010, 18). Independent reading is the time to see if your students are internalizing the CCSS and integrating them into their own strategic processing and reading work.

Richard Allington (2003) tells us that the more our students read, the better they read. As students spend significant time in independent reading, not only do they become better readers, developing their known vocabulary and their fluency as they read, but also build an ever-increasing repertoire of knowledge through extensive reading across multiple genres. Perhaps Dr. Seuss said it best when he said, "The more that you read, the more things you will know. The more that you learn, the more places you'll go." If we do not create opportunities for students to spend time reading at their independent level, when will they take on the important strategies we have modeled and demonstrated? When will they personally practice those strategies to develop flexibility and automaticity? How will they continue to encounter new knowledge, vocabulary, and reading challenges across a wide genre of text? Independent reading is the arena where everything students have worked toward comes to fruition; it is the students' chance to personally choreograph, rehearse, and solidify learned strategies and CCSS in their own reading

When students reach the *You Do* or independent phase of the gradual release model, they support themselves as readers and responders to text using what they have seen and practiced in the *I Do, We Do,* and *You Try* levels of gradual release. This last release of responsibility puts the reading work—this orchestration of strategies—into the students' hands. If we revisit Vygotsky's theories from Chapter 6, we see that the fourth phase represents the processing that occurs during independent reading. In this phase, the students develop flexibility and fluency with any learned strategies/standards, first incorporating them intentionally and then, with practice, automatically into their personal reading and thinking about text. The students integrate these new strategic pieces together with what they currently have under control to develop a self-extending system that they carry into any encounter with text across the school day and into their lives. Regie Routman (2003, 83) reminds us that as we independently read, we "use all these strategies at the same time, and our comprehension process is largely unconscious . . . ." Students must be able to use the strategy and, eventually, unconsciously and seamlessly apply it when they read (Routman 2003). This seamless weaving together of strategies and standards is facilitated when students spend ample, sustained time engaged in wide, voracious independent reading.

During the independent level of the gradual release of responsibility model, we strive to provide time for the practice necessary for students' reading strategies to evolve into the reading skills that are outlined in the CCSS.

Afflerbach, Pearson, and Paris (2008) describe strategies as goal-directed, intentional efforts by readers to solve problems such as decoding challenging text, deciphering word meaning, and comprehending as they read. When encountering a tricky part in text, strategic readers consciously and deliberately set about choosing a strategy to try out to fix the problem so they can move on. However, as students' inner control of a strategy becomes efficient, effective, and fluent, that strategy develops into a new skill that is applied when needed with speed and automaticity usually without the reader being aware of the components involved. Without significant amounts of purposeful practice on independent level text, students may not have enough successful experiences with reading to develop into skilled readers.

When matching texts to readers for effective independent practice, all of the faces of text complexity come into play—qualitative, quantitative, and reader/task considerations. As part of setting the stage for independent reading time, teachers demonstrate ways that students can best check a text to see if it is an appropriate one for them. One way that works for many students searching for a good fit text is to read several pages in the book and count on one hand how many "tricky" words they run across that they cannot read or comprehend. If there are five or more challenges on a page (fewer if there are fewer words on a page), then the text would likely be at a frustration level for the student. While there will indeed be opportunities for problem solving during independent reading, students should find most of the decoding or actual reading of the text very do-able. Teachers' concerns about text levels often center on the readability level, or the quantitative features of text. (See Chapter 3 for more information on text complexity.) However, we have found that many students are willing to attempt texts

> *When matching texts to readers for effective independent practice, all of the faces of text complexity come into play—qualitative, quantitative, and reader/task considerations. As part of setting the stage for independent reading time, teachers demonstrate ways that students can best check a text to see if it is an appropriate text for them.*

at higher quantitative levels when they are attracted to the qualitative features or they are interested in the characters, plot, concept, or topic of the text.

During independent reading, reader and task considerations play a significant role in motivating students to actively engage in reading over sustained periods of time. Comprehension improves when students are motivated and engaged in their reading and empowered by effective, strong reading instruction (Guthrie, Wigfield, and You 2010). Without motivation, many students buy out of independent reading, especially our below-level readers. There is a significant achievement gap between our strong readers who read avidly and our struggling readers who may read up to three times less than their classmates who are reading on grade level or above (Allington 2006). We want all of our students to choose to read and demonstrate the effective strategies, stamina, and interest to stick with it.

As stated previously, one way to ensure enhanced independent reading experiences for our students is help them find a good text match—one that they can really read and comprehend. Research also supports choice as a powerful motivating factor in getting students to read (Allen 2000; Allington 2002; Fountas and Pinnell 2001; Shapiro and White 1991). When students have the opportunity to select their own independent reading texts from a wide range of topics/themes, genres, and levels typically found in a classroom or school library, they often surprise us with their enthusiasm. Without input on their independent text selections, many students (and adults as well!) feel disenfranchised and unmotivated to read a text that does not meet their needs or interests (Cambourne 1995). Of course, from time to time, the teacher can choose to focus the students' independent practice on a particular genre such as poetry or biographies, yet within the featured texts available for independent reading, the students still have the opportunity to choose their own text from the collection.

We recognize that texts self-selected by the students for independent reading must also be "good fit" texts, meaning that the texts' complexity challenges but does not overwhelm the reader. Afflerbach, Cho, Kim, Crassas, and Doyle (2013) identify another important factor that can certainly impact students' motivation and success in their independent reading—self-efficacy. Students with self-efficacy believe that they have the capability to draw forth the strategic actions necessary to personally problem-solve a text challenge ("tricky part") and produce results. Students with high self-efficacy believe that with persistent effort, they can utilize the strategies they know to conquer and comprehend the text. Students with low self-efficacy have repeatedly encountered text that is too difficult for them, and therefore, they focus on their failures since the effort they expended and/or the strategies they tried during reading did not work for them. When students spend the majority of their time and effort decoding words in a text, they lose track of the text's meaning, and instead of becoming the fluent, skilled readers we are trying to build during independent reading, these students become frustrated word callers. Targeted CCSS-based small-group instruction for these students, focused on their successful engagement with text and effective strategic processing, fosters the development of self-efficacy that empowers and motivates these students as they move into independent reading.

During independent reading, students have the freedom to try out a text to see if it works within their level of strategic processing. Students may occasionally abandon a self-selected choice after reading a few pages if it does not interest them or if their reading itself becomes too labor-intensive for them to negotiate and construct meaning from. We conduct multiple conferences with individual students throughout the year to review their text selections. We monitor the complexity and levels of the text that the students read, specifically praising their current, effective reading work and nudging them to try out more challenging texts when appropriate. We talk to students about their interests and favorite authors or topics, and we suggest new texts to read. We support students as they set personal goals and search for text to achieve their goals. We encourage our students to explore different genres in their independent reading. We talk about what we are reading, and we continually pique our students' interest in new titles through short, fun book talks that leave them asking for more!

> During independent reading, students have the freedom to try out a text to see if it works within their level of strategic processing. Students may occasionally abandon a self-selected choice after reading a few pages if it does not interest them or if their reading itself becomes too labor-intensive for them to negotiate and construct meaning from.

Teachers spend time at the beginning of the school year setting up classroom procedures to foster positive independent reading experiences for students. Students need easy access to lots of text in order to maintain rigorous, engaged independent reading throughout the year. High-quality, well-organized classroom libraries provide most of the text for students to read during independent reading. (We believe that content-area teachers should have classroom libraries, too!) Gathering texts for these libraries can sometimes feel like a daunting and expensive task for the beginning teacher or teacher new to a grade level. Hopefully, your school recognizes the value of supporting teachers with a myriad of texts for their classroom libraries so that you "inherit" at least some titles when you move into a grade level. If you are starting from scratch, you can still create your own classroom library of independent-reading text. Begin with your school librarians. They are a great resource for building a collection of texts to get you started. Although this text must rotate back into the school library at some point, you can begin the year with some good text choices for students. School librarians often have back copies of student magazines that make great additions to a classroom library. Sometimes, your students' parents donate children's books that they no longer need at home. We discover great prices and selections at garage sales, library sales, parent-teacher organization book fairs, and discount used-book stores. We also purchase inexpensive copies of texts from book publishers who visit the school district during the year.

As you gather texts for your classroom library, be sure to reflect the wide range of text types represented in the CCSS. Include multimodal text (newspapers, menus, travel brochures, bookmarked web sites/pages), and use multimedia resources when available (iPad®, Kindle® readers, computers) to access text choices for students. Multigenre texts are critical building blocks for a classroom library. Ensure that your library includes at least 50 percent informational (nonfiction) texts across a wide range of topics and concepts. As you add to your classroom library each year, keep in mind this significant goal for independent reading that CCSS Introduction to the English Language Arts Standards presents: "Students who meet the standards readily undertake the close, attentive reading that is at the heart of understanding and enjoying complex works of literature. They habitually perform the critical reading necessary to pick carefully through the staggering amount of information available today in print and digitally. They actively seek the wide, deep, and thoughtful engagement with high-quality literary and informational texts that builds knowledge, enlarges experience, and broadens worldviews."

Teachers organize their classroom libraries in various ways. Most importantly, the text accessibility and organization have to make sense and work efficiently for you and your students. Some teachers like to let their students lead the organization process by selecting categories for sorting the texts for the classroom library. We know teachers who include this activity as part of their first week plans. Students get a hands-on preview of the texts to be included in the classroom library as they identify ways that the texts can be grouped into author sets, theme sets, topic sets, genre sets, etc. Colored-coded stickers or labels aligned to the various text collections are placed on the text back cover to help the students know where to reshelve the texts when they have finished reading. Other teachers choose to group texts by using qualitative readability levels (such as Lexile® levels referenced in the CCSS or guided reading levels). Students select good-fit independent reading text using the levels as a guide. This type of leveling in a classroom library seems to be effective with primary students as they are learning to read. Often, a collection of texts represents several consecutive levels (rather than one specific level), and this choice within a range of levels serves as enough of a support for students as they make their just-right text selections. Many teachers choose several ways to group and present the texts to the students. For example, a teacher may have some texts sorted by levels, some by topics, some as an author's set, and some by genre, such as fairy tales. Beth Newingham, a third grade teacher from Troy School District, graciously shares wonderful ideas for getting started in setting up a classroom library in her "Virtual Tour of Our Library" link on her website: http://hil.troy.k12.mi.us/staff/bnewingham/myweb3/index.htm. Find several sources such as the two provided above that present ideas for setting up classroom libraries, and then construct your library in a way that works for your students, resources, and space.

> *Many teachers choose several ways to group and present the texts to the students. For example, a teacher may have some texts sorted by levels, some by topics, some as an author's set, and some by genre, such as fairy tales.*

Many teachers, especially in elementary school, provide individual book bags or boxes to house each student's text choices for the week. We like to divide our elementary through middle school classes into five groups and assign a different day of the week for the students in each group to "go shopping" for independent reading texts, filling their book bags or boxes with their choices. This simple procedure minimizes students' wandering around the room to find a text and maximizes the time they spend in actual reading. Emergent readers include more text choices in their boxes/bags since the texts they read are much shorter than those of more experienced readers. These students need multiple texts to keep them engaged throughout the independent reading time. In addition, we ask the students to add the texts that they read in their small instructional reading groups to their boxes/bags. Teachers recognize that often, early readers read and reread their independent level texts during the week as these students continue to develop strategic control and fluency in their reading. With each reading, the students are freed up to notice new things about that text (Clay 1993).

Whether several students select to read a book from the same author and then gather together to share their responses or they are assigned a meaningful task to do after reading, we find that significant connections to previous learning are strengthened when students do something relevant and authentic after reading a text.

While there are times that our students read independently during class time for enjoyment, research suggests that accountability requirements keep students actively engaged during reading (Reutzel et al. 2010). In a study of highly effective reading teachers, Sherry Sanden, a professor at Illinois State University, found that those teachers believed that "inserting intentional opportunities for reading instruction and holding students accountable for the learning that ensues allows independent reading to hold increased possibilities for influencing their students' reading growth" (2012, 228). Whether several students select to read a book from the same author and then gather together to share their responses or they are assigned a meaningful task to do after reading, we find that significant connections to previous learning are strengthened when students do something relevant and authentic after reading a text. Providing students a choice of responses or tasks after reading an independent text is equally as motivating as allowing choice in text selection and enhances a sense of student ownership and engagement. In a study of fourth grade exemplary teachers (Allington 2002), observers noted that these teachers used longer tasks that gave students' time to read entire texts, involved multiple literacies and standards, allowed for individual and small group projects, and integrated several content areas. These longer undertakings proved more substantive and significant for students, leading to all students' engagement in complex responses to text. The performance tasks suggested in the CCSS Appendix B as well as those you design for your own students often require students to spend extended time in reading and responding based on the dimensions of the task. (See Chapter 4 for more on performance based tasks.) Independent reading time can be a perfect venue for students to dig into these reading performance tasks.

Robust academic conversations and intentional student interactions are essential to the independent reading context. Students share their thinking about the texts they have read and pondered. The Speaking and Listening Standards come alive as students engage in critical thinking, respond to the ideas of others, and co-construct new meaning. Whether students quickly share out in partnerships or triads at the end of an independent reading block, work together on a task in response to reading, or get together in small discussion groups, talk is reflection of student ownership of learning. Teachers can purposefully teach their students collaborative skills that enhance their academic conversations. These skills include such strategies as active listening, being responsible to your group, and supporting your findings or point of view (Harvey and Daniels 2009). Zwiers and Crawford (2011) introduce students to five skills to focus and deepen these student conversations: elaborate and clarify, support ideas with examples, paraphrase, build on and/or challenge ideas, and synthesize. In Zwiers and Crawford's book *Academic Conversations: Classroom Talk That Fosters Critical Thinking and Content Understandings*, teachers find a wide range of strategies to cultivate these powerful conversations across the school day, including the independent reading time. We find that when students employ effective speaking and listening skills along with real collaboration strategies as they dialogue together, we see an exciting addition to our independent reading block where students take ownership of their own talk about text.

The exemplary teachers observed by Allington nurtured talk that was "more conversational than interrogational . . . teachers and students discussed ideas, concepts, hypotheses, strategies, and responses with others. The questions teachers posed were more 'open' questions, where multiple responses would be appropriate" (Allington 2002). Often before independent reading, we ask students to read with a strategy goal in mind. We can also ask our students to read with several higher-level or open-ended questions in mind to focus their thinking. Even though they are reading different texts, after reading, students come together to talk about their texts and discuss their responses to the focus questions. For example, if our students are working on making inferences in a short story or novel, we might pose these questions before reading:

What is at least one theme that is emerging in your story? How does the main character reflect the theme you selected? How does the theme impact the main character? Explain your thinking.

At other times, we have a goal-setting conference with several students, and we ask them to read through the "lens" of a particular strategy or standard, practicing that focus as they read. When students touch base after reading, they share their thinking framed by that strategy/standard work. We might say to the class: *As you read today, if you get "stuck" and lose the meaning, see if rereading will get you back on track.*

Or we set this goal with several students:

You have been working on using text features in informational text to determine main ideas before and during reading. As you read one of your informational independent reading texts, think about how you use this strategy. Be ready to talk with your partner about the features in your text and if or how they supported your meaning-making as you read.

The framework for how independent reading looks varies from district to district and school to school. Some schools use school-wide, sustained silent reading (SSR) time, while other campuses utilize published computerized independent reading systems. Sometimes, even small reading group instruction can include an independent reading component when, after setting a focus for reading with the teacher, the students leave the group to read and respond to the text selection during independent reading and then return to the group for an instructional guided discussion about their reading. Keep in mind, however, that in this example, the text being read outside the small instructional group context must be at the students' independent level. Other teachers set up a read at home program to extend the time for independent reading outside the school day. Many teachers build independent reading into a reading workshop model. There are numerous ways to incorporate an independent reading time into your schedule. Consider the factors that we have talked about in this chapter, and then keep in mind that the best way for organizing independent reading for your classroom depends on your students' instructional strengths, their learning objectives, and their personal interests.

One extension of independent reading is the book club. Book clubs go by different names, and, depending on the teacher, reflect different designs. But the primary goal for all book clubs is the same—to get students excited about reading and talking about text. One interesting study, born from the frustration of teachers, students, and parents with their current computerized reading system, features a Book Bistro. Wendy Kasten and Lori Wilfong set up this study to see if establishing a Book Bistro, in place of the computerized program, would have an effect on students' attitudes toward independent reading in secondary classrooms (Kasten and Wilfong 2005). The study began with research that states that students are motivated to read when they talk about books (Adler, Rougle, Kaiser, and Caughlan 2004; Allington 2002; Au, Carroll, and Scheu 1997; Conniff 1993; Gambrell and Almasi 1996; Gambrell, 1996; Kasten, Kristo, and McClure 2005; Manning and Manning 1984). Since secondary students thrive on interpersonal relationships, tapping into the need for social interaction made sense. Believing that enthusiastic students breed eager readers, Kasten and Wilfong felt that the Book Bistro was an opportunity to keep students from feeling isolated during independent reading time. To start, all students selected their books for independent reading. The teachers made modifications for below-level readers by providing their book on audiotape so that these students could complete their reading in a timely fashion and be ready to meet with other students. In addition, the teachers searched for high-interest, low-readability books that these readers would want to read. Before the Book Bistro event, every student filled out an index card, giving information about the book they would be discussing. The teachers then used the cards to group students by their texts' genre and plot. During the event, the students gathered in small groups to interact and converse about their books, sharing answers to several intriguing questions about their reading, selected from a menu of questions. To create accountability as well as for grading purposes, the students assessed the engagement and responses of the person to their left and right. What Kasten and Wilfong found as a result of their Book Bistro study was a significant rise in students' reading success and their enthusiasm toward independent reading. Since this study, teachers extended Book Bistro into grades 2, 4, and 11, and they reported overwhelmingly positive results as well.

Bringing students together after reading an independent text to have relevant, targeted, and lively conversations about text or to engage them in purposeful, authentic performance tasks based on the text(s) they read creates a community of learners who support each other as they uncover the deeper meaning and ideas behind the text. We focus these discussions and tasks through the CCSS by crafting higher-order questions based on selected grade-level standards. Teachers or students can generate several questions to frame the independent reading time, or teachers can design a "menu" of questions. The students then select several questions from the menu to answer based on the text that they read during independent reading. The sample framework for the following menu questions draws directly from literature and informational text standards.

Literary Menu Questions after Independent Reading

(Book Club, Reading Partners, Share Circles, etc.)

Directions: Select one question from each section to talk about during book club.

Key Ideas and Details:

How does the main character change throughout the book? What clues at the beginning of the story foretell this transformation? Share brief sections from the book that illustrate this transformation.

What specific clues foreshadow what is to come in the story?

In what ways does the setting of the story impact the characters? How would things be different for the characters if the setting were different? Use the text to support your answers.

Craft and Structure:

Which details were critical for the author to include to carry the story forward to its conclusion?

At what points in the story did the author need the reader to read between the lines to figure out what was taking place?

A *motif* is a subject, theme, or idea. What motifs or distinctive patterns did you notice throughout the book? What was the author's intent in using these?

Integration of Knowledge and Ideas:

Read at least three reviews, chats, and/or synopses of this book from our bookmarked online source folder. How do these comments about the book differ from your impressions as a reader?

What background knowledge did the author need to be able to write this story? Where does he or she draw on other resources in the story? Share the sections where you found this to be true.

How does the main character in this story compare to the main character in another book you have read? Support your response with specific text examples from both books.

Informational Text Menu Questions after Independent Reading

(Book Club, Reading Partners, Share Circles, etc.)

Directions: Select one question from each section to talk about during book club.

Key Ideas and Details:

What are at least three key ideas presented in the text? How are these ideas significant to the topic of the text?

Select at least four text features from the text. How did these text features support the main idea of the text?

What is the main idea of this text? Which significant supporting details would be important to include in a summary of this text?

Craft and Structure:

What do you think is the author's intended message in writing this text? Justify your thinking, using text evidence.

From what point of view was this text written? How do you know? How does the author's point of view impact the presentation of the content?

What bias did you notice in the text? Show this, using text evidence.

Integration of Knowledge and Ideas:

What does the text tell us about the people and events during the time that it references? Support your answers with textual proof.

How do you know whether this text is accurate? Explain your answer, using text evidence from this text and other related documents.

What would be a more powerful way to present the information in the text? Explain your answer, using text evidence.

In crafting questions to spur students' thinking about their independent reading text, you hone specific questions to address your particular grade-level standards. As you begin to write your own menu of questions, start with the anchor standards and then look at your grade-level supporting standards. For example, Reading: Anchor Standard 3 is *Analyze how and why individuals, events, and ideas develop and interact over the course of a text.* The second grade supporting standard for literature is: *Describe how characters in a story respond to major events and challenges.* A second grade teacher might pose this question for students reading a fiction text to match the supporting standard: *Choose a big event from your book. How did each of the characters respond to this event? Why did they respond that way? Show examples from your story.*

The fifth grade supporting standard for this anchor standard is *Compare and contrast two or more characters, settings, or events in a story or drama, drawing on specific details in the text (e.g., how characters interact).* A fifth grade teacher might pose this question to match the supporting standard: *Select two important characters in your book. How do they compare to and contrast with each other? Show text evidence to support your answers.*

An 11th grade supporting standard for this anchor standard is: *Analyze the impact of the author's choices regarding how to develop and relate elements of a story or drama (e.g., where a story is set, how the action is ordered, how the characters are introduced and developed).* An 11th grade teacher might pose this question to match the standard: *Select two significant characters in the story. How does the author introduce these characters and develop them throughout the story? Use specific text evidence to illustrate the author's intentions.*

Notice that these questions (and often performance tasks based on supporting standards) may only address a portion of the standard. Careful analyzing of the total picture of each standard reinforces the fact that a teacher must model each of the elements of the standard, and students must practice the various dimensions of that standard again and again before students can achieve that standard's expectations at the independent level. The standards do not represent a checklist that students meet once and then move on to the next one. However, the complex, challenging goals of the CCSS are attainable through relevant, repeated scaffolded instruction, finally resulting in your students' strategy-to-skill development that evolves through much independent practice. "Simply put, students need enormous quantities of successful reading to become independent, proficient readers" (Allington 2002).

 ## Let's Think and Discuss

1. While the Speaking and Listening Standards are interwoven throughout the instructional day, how do these standards relate to the independent learning context in your classroom? Which procedures or structures do you (or could you) have in place to ensure that students have opportunities for meaningful conversations and interactions that incorporate these standards during independent activities?

2. How does this chapter help you begin to answer this question: "What are the rest of your students doing while you are working with small groups?"

Chapter 9

Writing Through the Lens of the CCSS

"Learn as much by writing as by reading"
—Attributed to Lord John Dalberg-Acton, 1834–1902

Teachers realize a perfect instructional context for integrating ELA standards when they incorporate purposeful writing into their students' literacy day. The Reading Standards along with the Language and Foundational Skills Standards articulate the interrelated role of these critical skills as students read and respond to text. Because reading and writing are reciprocal processes, these ELA Standards also work in partnership during writing. The decoding of reading links to the encoding of writing as seen in the kindergarten through fifth grade Foundational Skills Standards. The Language Standards, exemplified for students through mentor text examples and their own reading, are not isolated skills but instead are embedded into writing through the use of conventions, the consideration of vocabulary and word choice, and writing craft decisions. The Reading Standards set expectations for reading using analysis, research, and reflection (along with text evidence to support conclusions, opinions, and arguments) that are mirrored in many text types presented in the Writing Standards. Indeed, much of our students' reading work and assessment will most likely include written responses that reflect students' thinking about text. It is important to recognize that writing in the content areas is embedded into the kindergarten through fifth grade standards and expectations. Beginning in sixth grade, not only are writing standards found in ELA but also separate, but connected writing standards are included in the category, Grades 6–12 Literacy in History/Social Studies, Science, and Technical Subjects. Writing is a part of the entire school day, and the accountability for ensuring that students successfully meet the standards belongs to all teachers.

As we have seen in our previous chapters, the development of literacy is progressive, and the acquisition of reading strategies and skills solidly rests on a foundation of oral language through powerful academic conversations about text. From teacher read-aloud texts and directed model lessons to student shared interactive discussions and small-group engagements, purposeful talk shapes and enhances the meaning-making that students construct as they read. Yet "Reading *and* writing float on a sea of talk" (Britton 1983, 11). The Speaking and Listening Standards are essential to the writing process as students rehearse their ideas through talk before committing their words to paper. We note in Writing Standard 5 the importance of interactions with peers and adults to develop and strengthen writing through planning, revising, editing, and other writing processes. Our youngest writers learn that what they say can be written and what they write can be read. Through targeted conversations or conferences before and during writing, students share and firm up their thinking with a partner or a small group as they generate ideas, organize their thinking, review or expand their main points, check their meaning as they write, ask and respond to questions about their work, and revise their writing.

> *As we have seen in our previous chapters, the development of literacy is progressive, and the acquisition of reading strategies and skills solidly rests on a foundation of oral language through powerful academic conversations about text. From teacher read-aloud texts and directed model lessons to student shared interactive discussions and small-group engagements, purposeful talk shapes and enhances the meaning-making that students construct as they read.*

When examining the writing standards, we see that they fall into four clusters:

- Text Types and Purposes
- Production and Distribution of Writing
- Research to Build and Present Knowledge
- Range of Writing

Whereas the first three writing anchor standards, under Text Types and Purposes, focus on the types of writing or the "what to write," the next three writing anchor standards, under Production and Distribution of Writing, focus on the *how* of writing. In other words, these standards answer the question, *How should students write?* Standards 7–9 are centered on research and writing, while the Range of Writing Standard 10 articulates the how long and how often of writing.

Figure 9.1 The Writing Standards

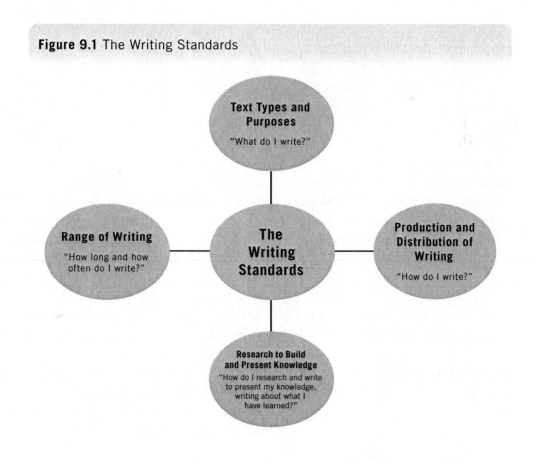

Before thinking about the text types outlined in the CCSS, we first examine the impact of the Range of Writing Anchor Standard (10) along with the standards of Production and Distribution of Writing (4–6) in our classrooms. Many teachers worry about the time commitment needed for students to master the writing standards. It *will* take time. Beginning in third grade, Standard 10 (under the Range of Writing) comes into play: *Write routinely over extended time frames (time for research, reflection, and revision) and shorter time frames (a single sitting or a day or two) for a range of discipline-specific tasks, purposes, and audiences.* Donald Graves (1994, 104) cautions, "If students are not engaged in writing at least four days out of five, and for a period of thirty-five to forty minutes, beginning in first grade, they will have little opportunity to learn to think through the medium of writing. Three days a week are not sufficient. There are too many gaps between the starting and stopping of writing for this schedule to be effective. Only students of exceptional ability, who can fill the gaps with their own initiative and thinking, can survive such poor learning conditions."

We believe that writing time in classrooms should not be hit or miss, but instead, a consistently scheduled routine that immerses students in the writing process. Students must develop texts in the course of one or two class periods or days, but they also write across longer time periods to author written texts that require research, depth of development, and revision to clarify meaning. Just as importantly, we see that time for writing happens across the curriculum for a variety of purposes and audiences. While Standard 10 is not a part of the writing standards in kindergarten, our kindergarten students build writing stamina during the year and they spend at least 15 to 20 minutes a day engaged in actually composing their own texts. By the end of the year, many of these students are even working on the same text across several days of writing time. The high expectations set forth in the CCSS for writing can only be accomplished by making writing time a scheduled priority in your classroom, beginning in the earliest grades.

The following Production and Distribution of Writing Anchor Standards focus on the processes and production of writing.

Standard 4. Produce clear and coherent writing in which the development, organization, and style are appropriate to task, purpose, and audience.

Standard 5. Develop and strengthen writing as needed by planning, revising, editing, rewriting, or trying a new approach.

Standard 6. Use technology, including the Internet, to produce and publish writing and to interact and collaborate with others.

As students grow as writers, they cultivate the ability to independently compose a text that is clear and well organized. Thus, Standard 4 tells us that students need to produce writing throughout the school year and the development and organization of the written texts must be appropriate to the writer's purpose and the task specifications (aligned with the stated grade-level expectations). While this standard begins in grade three, we find, once again, that our youngest writers can attend to writer's purpose and text organization as they build toward the full rigor of that standard in third grade. First graders amaze us by including organizational text features in their informational writing, such as a table of contents, several headings, a glossary, and even inset boxes explaining a vocabulary word they used in their text. Kindergartners compose letters to express their opinions about a decision to remove the monkey bars from the school playground. And second graders write articles for a school website to inform parents about the purpose of the local food bank and to solicit donations for a food drive the class chose to head up.

> As students grow as writers, they cultivate the ability to independently compose a text that is clear and well organized. Thus, Standard 4 tells us that students need to produce writing throughout the school year and the development and organization of the written texts must be appropriate to the writer's purpose and the task specifications (aligned with the stated grade-level expectations).

We find the foundation for establishing powerful writing instruction rests in fostering the development of the processes of writing presented in Standard 5. For teachers who are acquainted with writer's workshop, the processes named sound familiar—planning, developing, revising, rewriting, editing, etc. These writing processes evolve in sophistication across the grade levels with the continuing goal of students strengthening their written texts. If teachers already have an efficiently managed, rich writer's workshop in place, then they have a context established where they can effectively position instruction using the standards for their students. There are many authors who describe process writing and writer's workshop in detail, including how to set it up in your classroom (Donald Graves, Lucy Calkins, Ralph Fletcher, JoAnn Portalupe, Marcia Freeman, Regie Routman, and Nancy Atwell) Although the writing standards only present the "what" of writing, we personally feel that the writer's workshop is a solid stage upon which to choreograph the "how"—accomplishing the complex expectations of those standards. Students who know the procedures of writer's workshop and actively participate in the authoring cycle—planning, drafting (developing), revising, editing, publishing (rewriting, trying a new approach)—are set up with the tools that they need to dive into the challenges of the writing standards. Within the workshop or, if not using writer's workshop, the time set aside for writing, there must exist a carefully orchestrated, explicit sequence of instruction with multiple opportunities for students to practice all the writing types and receive critical feedback throughout the writing process (Calkins, Ehrenworth, and Lehman 2012).

Before we take a look at the text types and purposes presented in the writing standards, we need to consider how we best scaffold our support to help our students meet their challenges. Once again, we return to the superb pedagogy represented through the gradual release of responsibility as we move from focused teacher support—introducing and modeling the critical attributes, strategies, and crafting essentials for each writing type—to students taking control of this learning in their own writing. We begin with where the students are right now as writers. What are their current strengths? What do their written texts show that they understand about writing? Then, we need to closely peruse our grade-level writing standards. We need to also look at the writing expectations from the standards in previous years. How do our grade-level standards build upon the writing standards from previous years? In assessing where our students are as writers, we not only reflect on what they can do as writers based on former standards, but also look for gaps that students need filled or new learning that must occur in order to achieve this year's grade level writing standards. In addition, we like to look a grade-level up the ladder to see how the instruction we provide this year is essential to scaffold the students into the goals for the upcoming grade level. Familiarity with the writing standards both vertically between the grade levels and laterally across the year at your own grade level equips you to better scaffold your support for your writers.

Next, critically analyze the instructional essentials embedded within each standard as you plan your model lessons. This will first require you to deconstruct the overall standard by exploring the supporting grade-level standards. In grade 4 of the writing standards, we see that Standard 2 states: *Write informative/explanatory texts to examine a topic and convey ideas and information clearly.* When digging into that standard for fourth grade, we find that students must be able to do these things:

- Introduce a topic clearly and group related information in paragraphs and sections; include formatting (e.g., headings), illustrations, and multimedia when useful to aiding comprehension.

- Develop the topic with facts, definitions, concrete details, quotations, or other information and examples related to the topic.

- Link ideas within categories of information using words and phrases (e.g., another, for example, also, because).

- Use precise language and domain-specific vocabulary to inform about or explain the topic.

- Provide a concluding statement or section related to the information or explanation presented.

As we read each supporting standard with the understanding of where our particular students are as writers, we can see multiple model writing lessons (or mini-lessons) within each of these that may need to be presented, practiced, and then integrated into the students' writing before we can assess whether our students can effectively construct informational texts on a topic that clearly convey ideas and information. For example, in the first supporting standard above, we might model how to select a topic for informational writing based on purpose, interest, or the genre we will use for our written text. We need to talk about how to compose an effective lead for an informational text that introduces a topic clearly and draws the reader into the text. We model how to organize the facts, details, examples, etc. that we gather (see the second supporting standard) into meaningful paragraphs and sections to provide a cohesive flow in our informational writing. That action would also cause us to consider the third supporting standard as we transition between our ideas. We would use multiple published informational texts and multimedia to explore the effectiveness of a variety of text features and formatting choices in enhancing an author's meaning. We might demonstrate how we can incorporate several text features or multimedia into our own writing example. It is apparent that one quick model lesson will not be sufficient to present the depth and complexity represented in the supporting standards. We must break down each standard into its various critical components and demonstrate them in logical, small chunks for our students to then practice and explore in their own writing.

After teachers thoughtfully consider their model lessons for writing by selecting a specific doable teaching point that builds toward the writing standard, they demonstrate that teaching point using a personal or published writing example and think aloud how good writers employ this strategy or thought process in their own writing. Concrete examples along with teachers' "metacognitive" talk about the strategy or process provide the essential *I Do* support students need to see the writing work in action. Many teachers illustrate examples of powerful author's craft, using mentor or anchor texts that their students first encounter as readers to illustrate the featured writing focus. Dorfman and Cappelli (2007, 3) in their superb book *Mentor Texts: Teaching Writing Through Children's Literature, K–6*, tell us, "Mentor texts serve as snapshots into the future. They help students envision the kind of writer they can become; they help teachers move the whole writer, rather than each individual piece of writing, forward." (See also Dorfman and Cappelli's second book on mentor texts titled *Nonfiction Mentor Texts: Teaching Informational Writing Through Children's Literature, K–8*.) This tapping into text springboards students into trying on what they have seen exemplified in the mentor texts in their own writing. The authors of these mentor texts actually become our silent partners as we explore through our model lessons the attributes of different text types and what makes for good writing in order for students to write into the complexity of the standards.

After the *I Do* model lesson, the teacher invites the students to try out the new strategy or process in a shared, *We Do*, context. During this time, the students interactively negotiate a text where they practice the featured writing move. The teacher shares the pen with the students as they work together to compose a group exemplar text or illustrate the new strategy/process by using it in a current piece of writing they have constructed together. This community-developed text is usually written on chart paper or a white board so it is large enough for everyone to see what is written, revised, edited, etc. Students share ideas and reflections with partners and the group as they apply this new learning using the shared text in preparation to integrate it into their own writing practice.

The *You Try* phase of gradual release of responsibility to the students means that we give them ample time to write continuously on personal pieces of text. Students learn to write by writing and having daily opportunities to develop the necessary craft and skills supported by their teacher-coach. This is the level of scaffolding where writer's workshop comes into play as it represents guided writing practice. As students try out modeled and interactively practiced strategies, processes, and techniques in their own writing, teachers move about between the students and conference with them about their writing progress. Teachers take on many roles during this time. They often note and specifically name something for the writers that they are doing well. This directed feedback is essential to ensuring that the students continue effective practices. Teachers also probe to discern students' intent as they write, especially when they are trying to problem-solve or work through a tricky part in their writing. Teachers can ask questions about the students' writing or prompt them into consideration of possible "moves" they can make as an author. Teachers talk to students about their meaning as they write and help them clarify confusions. During the writer's workshop or guided writing time, teachers may revisit a model lesson with a student or a small group of students, or they may determine that one or two students are ready to take on something new in their writing that perhaps the other students have not yet encountered. In that case, the teacher can do a quick model of the strategy, let the students

> *This directed feedback is essential to ensuring that the students continue effective practices. Teachers also probe to discern students' intent as they write, especially when they are trying to problem-solve or work through a tricky part in their writing. Teachers can ask questions about the students' writing or prompt them into consideration of possible "moves" they can make as an author.*

try it out in interactive practice with the teacher or another student, and then move it into their own writing. Carl Anderson, in his book *How's It Going?: A Practical Guide for Conferring with Student Writers,* provides teachers many ideas for supporting students' guided writing practice through effective conferences that accelerate students' writing growth (2000). At the end of the writer's workshop, students often debrief their writing with a partner and set goals for the next time they write. The *You Try* guided practice writing time is essential for building students' academic optimism and perseverance as well as solidifying what they can now do as writers.

Students encounter ample occasions during the school day when they will be asked to write independently. Without opportunities for learning how to write effectively that are provided through the *I Do, We Do,* and *You Try* phases of gradual release, students do not have the tools or skills that they need to continue to grow as writers. When independent writing follows instructional and practiced writing, students demonstrate increasing control and sophistication both in their writing skills and in their writing content. Whether students are writing about their problem-solving in math or recording their hypotheses, data, procedures, and conclusions in science, or constructing an argument and defending their position in a history class, or analyzing the evolution of a character throughout a novel, or responding to an assessment task, the impact of their content depends on the quality of their writing. Content-area teachers support their students before they compose a subject-specific text for the first time (such as a science journal or social studies document-based question response) by incorporating what the students already know about writing from previously scaffolded instruction and then walking students through the phases of gradual release to demonstrate and develop the processes, attributes, and content necessary for writing the required content-area text. Creating independent opportunities for students to compose text ensures that they continue to grow in writing fluency, confidence, and flexibility as they address a variety of writing prompts, text types, and purposes.

A quick look at the last standard under Production and Distribution of Writing confirms that technology is entrenched in today's writing process. From providing sources for research to serving as a tool for publication and creative presentation, technology is essential and motivating for the 21st century learner. The range of what student writing can look like when blended with technology is only limited by the opportunity to use these resources. We are excited about tapping into the technology potential that will broaden the horizons of what our students can accomplish as writers.

The Text Types and Purposes Anchor Standards for Writing outline three text types: argument texts, informative/explanatory texts, and narrative texts. By 11th and 12th grade, the Text Types and Purposes CCSS Writing Anchor Standards are as follows:

Standard 1. Write arguments to support claims in an analysis of substantive topics or texts, using valid reasoning and relevant and sufficient evidence.

Standard 2. Write informative/explanatory texts to examine and convey complex ideas and information clearly and accurately through the effective selection, organization, and analysis of content.

Standard 3. Write narratives to develop real or imagined experiences or events using effective technique, well-chosen details, and well-structured event sequences.

The expectations for these text types and purposes evolve in complexity from kindergarten to 12th grade. When examining the Text Types and Purposes Anchor Writing Standards from third grade on, we discover that almost all of the supporting standards found in the CCSS Writing Standards fall under these first three Writing Anchor Standards. The supporting standards describe the critical dimensions that combine to define the complexity of that anchor standard at a particular grade level. To view grade level exemplars of each of these text types along with an annotation of what the student can do based on the writing standard, refer to Appendix C of the CCSS.

Let's examine each text type individually. We begin with the narrative text since teachers and students tend to be more familiar with this type of writing. The CCSS Appendix A, page 23, defines narrative writing: *Narrative writing conveys experience, either real or imaginary, and uses time as its deep structure. It can be used for many purposes, such as to inform, instruct, persuade, or entertain.* A sense of narrative text develops early on as students in school are exposed to a myriad of fiction texts. Teachers plant the language of story in students' ears as teachers read aloud numerous picture books and short stories. Each of these texts becomes a mentor text, with the authors modeling for students their craft of writing narrative text such as using effective leads and conclusions, developing powerful characters through dialogue and inner thoughts, incorporating unique plots with a variety of conflicts, describing settings, and employing interesting sentence structures, word choice, and imagery. Classroom teachers can easily piggyback many of the Reading: Literature

CCSS into an exploration of author's craft, using reading text excerpts to show students how expert authors incorporate key features of narrative text into their writing.

While the narrative writing standard does not include some creative forms of writing, most notably poetry, the range of narrative texts includes memoirs, autobiographies, fictional stories, anecdotes, accounts of historical figures and events such as in social studies, procedural descriptions that students followed in a science investigation, and other texts of a narrative nature (see CCSS Appendix A, 23–24). Students may take "compositional risks" from time to time and embed narrative writing elements into other writing types, such as the student who writes an informational piece on race cars and at the same time effectively interjects a personal anecdote about his visit to a race track.

For many years, we have started our writing time with a model lesson for our students explaining how we generate ideas for Stories Inside Me. It is commonly accepted that students usually write best about what they know, which makes this personal memoir a successful starting point for our writing year. In the beginning, we attempt to capture on our own "Stories Inside Me" list those significant, small moments from our lives to write about instead of a huge topic like "My Summer Vacation." One such list from a primary teacher includes ideas for narrative text such as, *the jellyfish sting; losing my dog, Maggie; and the log ride.* These are phrases to call to mind our stories, not titles for our stories. When modeling how to generate ideas for older students, one teacher's memoir topics include *the bully, getting to drive on my 16th birthday, and summer camp challenge.*

We use our first narrative piece to carry students through the gradual release of responsibility while modeling and practicing the writing process and procedures for the year. Students compose their first narrative text during writer's workshop, and we take every student through to publishing their text so they can experience the full breadth of the writing process. We assess our students as writers as they work, and we determine where they currently stand in relationship to the narrative writing standard/supporting standards as well as any applicable grade-level Foundational or Language Standards. We thoughtfully select teaching points for initial model lessons that set the parameters for our writing time and start to move students forward as writers. We include grade-level, standards-based crafting lessons for composing narrative text such as how to use dialogue to give insight into the narrator and other characters as well as conventions lessons (see the Language Standards) such as how to punctuate that dialogue. What we teach arises directly from what the students demonstrate that they need or are ready to take on next in their writing.

Approximately one-third of the overall time set aside during the year for writing is devoted to students writing narrative texts. (The rest of the time is split between composing informational/explanatory texts and opinion/argument texts.) Depending on the grade level, the students' understanding of narrative text types expands as they move from memoirs and anecdotes to drafting fictional stories or content-area narratives. With each successive narrative writing experience, students display a growing control over the elements of this text type. With daily targeted model lessons (mini-lessons), opportunities for shared and guided practice, and writing conferences about their progress, students effectively produce quality narrative text.

> *With daily targeted model lessons (mini-lessons), opportunities for shared and guided practice, and writing conferences about their progress, students effectively produce quality narrative text.*

Another text type specified in the writing standards is informational/explanatory text. The CCSS ELA Appendix A defines this text type.

> *Informational/explanatory writing conveys information accurately. This kind of writing serves one or more closely related purposes: to increase readers' knowledge of a subject, to help readers better understand a procedure or process, or to provide readers with an enhanced comprehension of a concept.*

Informational/explanatory writing provides the reader with information about a topic that is drawn from the writer's background knowledge and outside primary or secondary sources. To us, A. D. Van Nostrand (1979) captures the essence of informational/explanatory writing: "Composing consists of joining bits of information into relationships, many of which have never existed until the composer utters them. Simply by writing—that is, by composing information—you become aware of the connections you make,and you thereby know more than you knew before starting to write. In its broadest sense, knowledge is an awareness of relationships among pieces of information. As you compose, your new knowledge is your awareness of those relationships." In writing informational texts, students collect information, build new knowledge, sort and structure it into meaningful relationships, and, in doing so, actually become "experts" on their selected topic.

Multiple writing genres fall under informational/explanatory texts including summaries of texts read, literary analyses, science lab reports, movie or book descriptions, feature news articles, science and history reports, and functional writing (memos, instructions, resumes, etc.). According to Appendix A (23), informational/explanatory writing addresses relationships and matters such as:

1. types *(What are the different types of Shakespearean plays?)* or components *(What makes a good speech?)*

2. size *(How big is a germ?)*, function *(What are tooth keys used for?)*, or behavior *(Why do sharks attack people?)*

3. how things work *(How does a solar lamp work?)*

4. why things happen *(Why do tides occur in the ocean?)*

As with narrative writing, students need to have the time to work through the writing process to learn how to write effective informational text. Teachers design focused model lessons to introduce different genres of informational writing and the standards that are specific to this type of writing. During writer's workshop, students plan and develop drafts that they rethink and revise, using feedback from teachers and peers, to eventually produce well-crafted texts. Once again, the role of mentor texts cannot be underestimated. Teachers draw students' attention to the language and features of published informational texts and draw students into conversations about the authors' craft. Students begin to incorporate many of the same ideas and features in their own writing and progress in their ability to aptly develop their topics or themes using well chosen concrete details, examples, specific facts, quotations, and eventually citations. Teachers intentionally plan for informational writing instruction guided by their grade-level targets for this text type. They also carefully note the progression of skills that lead up to their grade level to assess where their students are in relationship to the previous standards from the grade levels below. The CCSS clearly demonstrate that both ELA and content-area teachers share the responsibility for the inclusion of this text type in their instruction. Students work through the writing process to learn and practice how to author informational text and then purposefully apply what they have taken when writing throughout the content areas.

Informational writing explains the why or how concerning a topic and seeks to clarify information. But informational writing differs from argument writing in that it does not seek to prove a point or change people's minds about a topic.

Informational mentor texts illustrate probably the most critical feature of this text type for students: text structure. The CCSS requires that students organize this informational writing into a deliberate structure. Teachers can find a plethora of mentor texts in their own classrooms or school libraries to exemplify a variety of text structures for students including descriptive/ enumerative, chronological, question/answer, problem/solution, compare/ contrast, and cause/effect. Teachers provide students ample opportunities to dig into the structural design of these texts, noticing the presentation and organization of ideas, the ways authors support their topic with evidence, the elaboration of details, the use of text features, and any other writing expertise demonstrated. Often, teachers create a physical "map" of the structure of a text or short text chunk, using a graphic organizer or thinking map that represents that structure. This map provides a visual for students so they can see the underpinnings of a text's organization. For example, details placed onto a Venn diagram represent how an author uses a compare/contrast text structure. A web provides a possible model for a descriptive text. As students dive into their topic or theme using carefully chosen details and text evidence, they make decisions on how to organize that information into a just right text structure that fits their desired presentation for their topic or theme.

Informational writing explains the *why* or *how* of a topic and seeks to clarify information. But informational writing differs from argument writing in that it does not seek to prove a point or change people's minds about a topic. While the CCSS scaffold opinion writing in grades kindergarten through five into argument writing for grades six through twelve, there is no denying that the argument text type holds a unique place in the standards. In fact, Appendix A, page 24, tells us, "While all three text types are important, the standards put particular emphasis on students' ability to write sound arguments on substantive topics and issues, as this ability is critical to college and career readiness." In addition, the standards delineate the critical attributes of argument writing as opposed to persuasive writing in this way: "A logical argument, on the other hand, convinces the audience because of the perceived merit and reasonableness of the claims and proofs offered rather than either the emotions the writing evokes in the audience or the character or credentials of the writer" (Appendix A, 24). We see the text evidence so essential to thinking and responding in the reading standards echoed here in the necessity to support opinions and arguments with reasonable and credible proof. This expectation means that as students move up in the grade levels they will eventually use and evaluate sources, deeply analyze source evidence to develop sound arguments, and refute alternate or opposing claims.

Standard 1's placement in the Text Types and Purposes seems to stress the CCSS view of the importance of being able to form and support opinions and arguments through writing. To learn to effectively argue through writing is a step-by-step process and, although the supporting standards for each grade level rise quickly in complexity, instruction must begin in a simple manner beginning with the youngest writers. In grades kindergarten through five, students compose opinion pieces. Opinion writing in grades kindergarten through five is the precursor to argument text types. Elementary students still must use text evidence to support a well-stated opinion about a text or topic. We can ask kindergarten grade students to choose their favorite Eric Carle book and use relevant details from the book to support their opinion. Second graders working with their art teacher write their opinion about who is their favorite artist after reading biographical picture books about several noted artists and viewing samples of their work. Students in fifth grade express their opinion about global warming based on several informational texts the class reads as well as interviews and multimedia sources. In all three examples, these elementary students are going back to the text, using facts and details to support their opinions.

When opinion writing "grows up" through the writing standards, it matures into argument writing. In an argument text type, students include evidence to support their claims, and examine opposing sides to their claims. They must examine the strengths and limitations of each position and "draw evidence from literary or informational texts to support analysis, reflection, and research" (Standard 9). Argument writing is used in many contexts, but its goals are either to get the reader to change his or her mind, to get the reader to act, or get the reader to acknowledge the position of the writer. In ELA, students may defend literary interpretations of meaning using argument texts. In social studies or history, they may argue an interpretation of a historical event after analyzing conflicting views presented through primary sources, texts, and multimedia references. In science, data, evidence, and other resources provide support for students' claims in response to questions or hypotheses. Once again, we see the ownership for bringing students up to the complexity of these argument writing standards belongs to both the ELA and the content-area teachers.

Because of the challenges presented by opinion/argument writing standards, teachers will find the need to proceed slowly and purposefully in planning their model lessons for this text type, allowing ample time for shared practice and providing guided practice along with supportive feedback through conferencing during writer's workshop. Analyzing the text structure, claims, and evidence seen in mentor texts gives students examples of how to construct effective arguments that they can attempt in their own writing. We suggest that you incorporate multiple shared encounters with constructing this text type with your students. Work with your students to interactively talk through and negotiate a plan for writing and then compose a shared opinion/argument class text, developing a position and supporting claims on a topic that is relevant and highly interesting for your students. Examine together the unique skills attributed to this text type, while celebrating all the great things that your students already know about writing that can help them craft their text.

The last Writing Anchor Standards to examine are Standards 7, 8, and 9—the Research to Build and Present Knowledge standards. By grades 11–12, these standards have "grown up" and state:

Standard 7. Conduct short as well as more sustained research projects to answer a question (including a self-generated question) or solve a problem; narrow or broaden the inquiry when appropriate; and synthesize multiple sources on the subject, demonstrating understanding of the subject under investigation.

Standard 8. Gather relevant information from multiple authoritative print and digital sources, using advanced searches effectively; assess the strengths and limitations of each source in terms of the task, purpose, and audience; and integrate information into the text selectively to maintain the flow of ideas, avoiding plagiarism and overreliance on any one source and following a standard format for citation.

Standard 9. Draw evidence from literary or informational texts to support analysis, reflection, and research.

The research standards are inexorably linked to the reading standards, and elements of these standards are embedded into all three text types. We easily see the impact of these standards on writing argument and informational texts. Standard 9 focuses on writing in response to reading, either literary or informational, and again emphasizes the essential skill of writers (and readers) to support all thinking and research with credible text evidence and, eventually, text evidence from a variety of sources. The CCSS recognizes that research projects can be short or long in nature, include multiple literacies, and can be integrated into any part of the curriculum.

Since reading and writing are reciprocal processes, we can link Standard 9 in writing—*Draw evidence from literary or informational texts to support analysis, reflection, and research*—with standard 9 in Reading: Literature—*Analyze how two or more texts address similar themes or topics in order to build knowledge or to compare the approaches the authors take.* Using these two standards as our focus (although many other standards come into play with this example), we ask our third grade students to respond to this prompt: Using specific examples from at least three texts, answer this question: Based on the text that you read, what does it mean to be a friend? As you reflect on your reading before you write, think about which characteristics the friends in the books you read seem to have in common. What evidence can you find in the characters' actions or their dialogue that demonstrates what makes a good friend? The students navigate through the writing process as they conduct their personal research on this question. The teacher breaks down the task into "doable" tasks, perhaps modeling how to take notes or mark significant text proof/examples with sticky notes, or, in another lesson, brainstorms with students a list of character traits that would make for a good friend based on examples from a story that they have read together as a class. After the students have read the three texts that they choose from a text set centered on friendship (such as *Frog and Toad Are Friends* by Arnold Lobel, *Bink and Gollie* by Kate DiCamillo, and *The Red Book* by Barbara Lehman), the students plan and begin to draft their writing. The teacher continues model lessons before each writer's workshop session to support students as they write, thinking aloud and demonstrating key points such as how to organize their writing or how to support their analysis of friendship traits with text examples. In the same way, older students in a history class can read primary sources concerning slave life such as the *Narrative of the Life of Henry Box Brown*, examine various slave poster advertisements, and peruse newspaper excerpts from William Lloyd Garrison's newspaper, *The Liberator*, and then respond to their research by writing an analysis of these three accounts and what they tell us about the people living in that time in history.

The following is an example of a second grader's "research writing" based on her investigations into the life of her favorite mammal—the raccoon. This student read two books and a science magazine article on raccoons, and she watched a short online video about raccoons. She next planned, wrote, and published her research during writer's workshop over the course of a week. She edited her writing with the teacher in an editing conference. Then, the edited text was typed by an adult for publication, but the words and illustrations belong completely to the author. We can almost hear the many model lessons this young writer has taken on and used in her text. Most interestingly, this author took a compositional risk and wrote her piece through the voice of the raccoon after hearing her teacher read aloud a mentor text written from the point of view of an animal.

Figure 9.2 Second Grade "Research Writing" Example

Remarkable Raccoons

How would you like to spend most of your life in a tree? That's what I do! Some of my friend raccoons also live in grasslands. We have been found in cities, and we might live in your chimney. Some people put nets on their chimneys to keep us out, but they have never caught me!

I am a mother raccoon, and I take good care of my babies. I carry my babies in my mouth, not on my back. Baby raccoons are called cubs. My babies copy me to learn how to survive. When my baby raccoons learn to climb a tree, they have to practice a lot.

Raccoons explore for food for a long time. While we look for food, we might just take a nap. Good food for raccoons is grapes, snails, and birdseed. We can grab a fish as quick as a blink of an eye! Sometimes, we may also eat garbage—yuk!

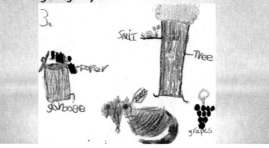

> Raccoons better watch out for enemies! Our enemies are the wildcat, fox, and coyote. Because we are clever and look like we wear a fur mask, many children think we are special animals. And, don't you think it would be fun to live in a tree?

The frontier of writing instruction and student engagement in the writing process stands mapped before us through the CCSS Writing Standards. This adventure is a shared experience with every teacher in every content area. Just as in any journey, we must carefully study the trail and understand the tools and skills that we need to equip ourselves and those who travel with us. Our job is to construct a clear route and plan our time wisely to meet all of our expectations and ensure that our students successfully reach the goals set forth. The potential that comes from teaching writing well and providing our students time to learn to write lies in our hands as teachers. We can start slowly if we are new to teaching writing, but as we hit our stride, we realize that we have the capability to build a writing community with our students that grows effective, confident authors.

> *The frontier of writing instruction and student engagement in the writing process stands mapped before us through the CCSS Writing Standards. This adventure is a shared experience with every teacher in every content area. Just as in any journey, we must carefully study the trail and understand the tools and skills that we need to equip ourselves and those who travel with us.*

Let's Think and Discuss

1. How can you effectively integrate the Writing Standards 7, 8, and 9 (the Research Standards) with your reading instruction? How can these standards relate to students' content area instruction in science or social studies?

2. As you consider the Writing Standards and the content of this chapter, think about writing with your own students. Which of the standards do you feel are the most successful in your classroom? Why? Which standards do you find the most challenging? Why? How might you begin to address those standards in your instruction?

Chapter  10

Bringing It All Together

> *Skills—whether about decoding, comprehension, fluency, language, writing, genre, whatever—are nothing more than a means to an end; they are not ends unto themselves. Their worth equals their contributions to reading and writing growth and text understanding.*
>
> —P. David Pearson 2004, slide 12

Back in 2004, before there were Common Core State Standards, P. David Pearson made the statement above at an international conference. In the same presentation, he urged educators to merge authentic student activity and "ambitious instruction" into a powerful curriculum that provides "skills that give kids independence, writing opportunities that promote their communicative competence, and reading opportunities that promote engagement, motivation, and intellectual challenge" (Pearson 2004, slide 74). This same commentary seems just as applicable today as we attempt to ensure that our students receive a rigorous, challenging curriculum delivered by empowered teachers immersed in effective pedagogy and focused on successful student literacy learning.

The Common Core State Standards in English Language Arts frame the *what* of our curriculum. As teachers, we must have within our repertoire a plethora of strategies built on sound research and practice to drive the *how* of planning for and delivering targeted, engaging, and effective instruction toward these standards. Based on research from 1998, it was noted that if teachers set aside 30 minutes to teach each identified state and/or national content standard or benchmark from elementary school through high school, it would take about nine more years of school for students to learn them all (Marzano and Kendall 2000; Tomlinson and McTighe 2006). What a daunting task for educators! As we examine the multiple standards and supporting standards in ELA across Reading: Literature, Reading: Informational Text, Writing, Language, Speaking and Listening, and, for elementary, Foundational Skills, we acknowledge that students have a monumental and complex "staircase" of learning to surmount each year. Even though we now have the CCSS to guide us, we continually consider how to best meet the rigorous demands of the standards within the confines of our instructional year. This goal is best met when we thoughtfully ponder how the standards interplay through our "ambitious instruction" and how we integrate them into carefully orchestrated, authentic tasks for our students.

When you think about how the CCSS impact your instructional decisions and resulting student engagement in this literacy work, always begin with your grade-level specific standards and then reflect on how a variety of standards, both grade-level standards and previous standards, naturally come together as students engage with text through reading and writing. While you may have a particular standard as your main teaching focus, likely a multitude of other standards underpin your lesson and your students' interactions during the learning. Therefore, many of the standards (and supporting standards) are addressed intentionally—and sometimes even incidentally—as students engage in powerful, connected reading and writing experiences. Add in some content-area reading and writing during both the ELA time and subject-specific instruction, and all at once, through careful planning, the standards intertwine and become quite doable through multiple encounters and contexts during the school year.

> *Even though we now have the CCSS to guide us, we continually consider how to best meet the rigorous demands of the standards within the confines of our instructional year.*

We always appreciate a few models to help us envision how the content covered in a professional book comes together in actual classroom instruction. All the good pedagogy—the how—that we have discussed within this book comes into play in the following examples; the CCSS require this from us. If we want our students to meet the complexity of these standards, we must build our instruction in a comprehensive, purposeful, integrated manner centered on the standards and then carefully monitor that instruction, watching for the intended results. Together, all of our focused effort and instructional expertise *will* bring our students— your students—to that level of deep understanding and higher-order thinking called for within the CCSS.

As you read the following examples, keep the appropriate grade-level CCSS ELA Standards at hand. (And for the middle school example, also have the ELA History/Social Studies Standards available.) We only identify for you one main teaching focus in each of the two examples. After you read the lessons, scan the standards/supporting standards for each exemplar grade level and see how many of them are actually encompassed in the lessons. You may be surprised how seamlessly these teachers enveloped multiple standards into their instruction.

Elementary School Example

A second grade teacher previews her teaching focus based on the CCSS and cross-checks the students' readiness for the standards she selects with a preassessment and informal observations in order to ascertain the just-right entry level for her instruction on the standard(s). In this case, the teacher plans her primary focus on word meaning based on several combined Reading and Language Standards: *Students describe how words and phrases contribute to meaning in a story, an informational text, and a poem and demonstrate an understanding of word relationships or nuances in word meaning.* She selects two read-aloud texts and a close reading of a poem to model the focus and provide shared practice. She intends to extend the students' practice through small-group instruction and independent reading. Finally, she will wrap up the experience with the students using descriptive language to write an individual composition (either a short informational text or an informational poem).

Because the students are also studying animal diversity in science, the teacher chooses three texts about fireflies for her lesson. The first text is a fiction text titled *Fireflies* by Julie Brinckloe (1985). The second text is a grade-level informational text about fireflies. The last text is a poem by Paul Fleischman called "Fireflies," excerpted from *Joyful Noise: Poems for Two Voices* (This poem is found in its entirety in the CCSS, Appendix B, page 52). The teacher also creates a few PowerPoint slides with photographs of fireflies (and some background music) to open her lesson.

As the students gather on the rug in the reading area, the teacher tells her students to quietly view the slides of fireflies. When the presentation is finished, she asks the students to share their observations with a buddy sitting near them. The teacher drops in on several partnerships to listen to their conversations (a process that she continues throughout the lesson whenever the students share between themselves). She hears many personal stories about the students' experiences with fireflies as well as conversations about how cool fireflies are when they light up. Then, the teacher requests that the students view the slides one more time and, this time, think about words that describe the fireflies or what they are doing. Once again, the students share their thinking with their partners. The teacher jots down some of the words that they suggest on large index cards, one word per card, and places the words in a large pocket chart. The students read the words together. They talk about how some of the words describe how the fireflies look and some tell what the fireflies do. They sort the words into two groups based on these reflections—describing words, or "awesome adjectives," and action words, or "vivid verbs"—terms that they have learned in prior lessons. There are three word cards that tell about parts of the firefly—*antennae, wings, light*—so the students decide to make one more group of naming words, or "on-the-nose nouns."

Next, the teacher reads the book *Fireflies* to her students. As she reads, she asks the students to think about the words that the author uses to really paint a picture of fireflies in the reader's mind. The students have done this type of activity many times before, and they are ready to explore the author's word choice. The teacher stops several times to reread a chunk of text and comment on her thinking about the author's language. She also stops several times to let the students share out some of the word choices that they think are particularly effective.

At the conclusion of the story, the teacher first gives the students time to react to the content of the text and talk about what they noticed. They especially want to talk about why the boy chose to let the fireflies go. The teacher then writes on cards any words that the students identified to describe the fireflies and their actions. The students help her sort the cards into the three groups. Several students are excited that they mentioned some of the same words that Brinckloe used in her book. The students read the words from each group and discuss which words they think best help them "picture" fireflies.

The teacher now shares an informational text about fireflies. She reads several pages and then lets students discuss some of the facts they heard about fireflies. She especially focuses on two pages that describe the special trait of bioluminescence and how fireflies use their light to attract mates. The teacher asks the students how this author used special word choice to help the reader picture details about the fireflies. The students choose several words to add to the pocket chart. Of course, they want to have the long six-syllable word *bioluminescent*!

At the conclusion of the lesson, each student is given a large sticky note. They write an informational sentence about a firefly, using at least two words from the cards on the word chart. The students read their sentences to the class as the teacher comments on their great word choice and how effectively their words painted a picture in the reader's mind.

On the second day, the teacher continues to focus on the meaning of words and phrases using a close reading of the poem "Fireflies." The poem is displayed on a chart or projected onto a screen. The teacher elicits the support of another teacher or older student to be the second "voice" for the first dramatic reading of the poem to the students. After the students hear the poem, they turn to a partner and share their responses to the content. The teacher drops in and listens to their comments, probing their thinking with questions. The students then share out their thoughts with the group. The teacher has several questions prepared if she needs to prime the students' thinking pumps.

➯ Why did the poet write this poem this way? Why are there two speakers?

➯ What do the speakers in the poem know about real fireflies? Why do you think that?

➯ What are the speakers' feelings about fireflies? How do you know?

The teacher is thrilled when several students immediately note that the talking back and forth in the poem and word repetition is like the flashing of the fireflies back and forth in the dark. They even use their new word, *bioluminescent*. The students like the comparison that fireflies are like writers. Many students point out all the rhyming words. Some of the students notice that there are many words in the poem that begin with *f* or *fl*. The teacher discovers that the students guide the majority of this first discussion with their comments, and she only needs to extend their thinking from time to time.

Now the teacher is ready for a second reading of the poem. She asks the students to think about the mind pictures that the poet creates with his word choices. She divides the students into two groups to represent the two voices in the poem. The students read the poem back and forth between the voices as the teacher and her helper read and point to the words. After the students share-read the poem, the teacher tells them that there are a few hard words in the poem that the reader needs to understand to grasp the deep meaning of the poem. The teacher uses a picture and a kid-friendly definition to help students understand the meaning of *parchment*. The group goes back and reads the section with this word, and they talk about how the light of the fireflies is like ink on the black paper of the night. The teacher directs a similar process with the words *calligraphers*, *penmanship*, and the phrase *fleeting graffiti*. Then the group rereads the poem.

The teacher poses several of these questions for the students to discuss with their partners and then share out with the group:

- ➨ Which words or phrases did the poet use to help you make mind pictures (images) of the fireflies? (The students add any new words to cards for the pocket chart.)

- ➨ How do those mind pictures help us understand the actions of fireflies?

- ➨ How do the mind pictures of the fireflies that the poet creates make the fireflies seem like people?

- ➨ What does the poet want the reader to think about fireflies? How do you know?

- ➨ How is this poem like the two books we read? How is it different?

To complete this day's lesson, the teacher and students work together to negotiate the text for a short paragraph about fireflies. They focus on incorporating words or phrases from their word cards as they write an informational description of fireflies. The teacher "shares the pen" with different students as the students work together to compose the text on a group chart. The teacher holds students accountable for what they already know about writing sentences, using high-frequency words, breaking words into chunks to spell them, and other applicable foundational skills and writing conventions. The students reread the text frequently as they write together another text that incorporates some of their new vocabulary.

During the next week, the teacher moves the teaching focus into small group instruction. Based on where students are as readers, she places them in four groups to read two good-fit paired texts in a guided small group context. Each group has a literary text (story or poem) and an informational text on the same topic. (The topics selected are *bees*, *butterflies*, and *ants*.) The teacher meets with the groups as the students read the two texts and talk about the important facts and details presented. The teacher serves as a scribe and works with each group to create a graphic organizer that identifies some of the significant facts from their texts about their insect. Then, the students work together to collect and record at least 10 words or short phrases that are used in the texts and effectively create mind pictures for the reader.

Finally, the students choose to write a short informational text or an informational poem about their insect. They focus on including important details about their insect, using words that create descriptive mind pictures. They have both their group's graphic organizer and word charts to use as tools as they write. The teacher conducts several model lessons during the writing process depending on the students' needs, such as how to write an effective lead for an informational text. She is pleased that four students choose to write a poem, and she meets several times with these students to talk about ways they can organize or format their poem. One student, inspired by Fleischman, writes a poem titled "Bees: A Poem for a Buzzy Voice." Needless to say, he uses a lot of onomatopoeia!

The teacher conducts individual revision conferences with her students, and the students confer frequently with their writing partners. The students use a revision rubric and a familiar class editing checklist to prepare their writing for publishing, and then they sign up for an editing conference with the teacher. The experience ends with each student publishing their writing with illustrations. Together, they celebrate their success by reading their personal favorite descriptive sentences or poetry lines—mind pictures—from their work.

1. How did the primary teaching focus echo throughout the four to five days of instruction?

2. While there was a primary focus, the teacher had many other standards intentionally in play as she planned her instruction. Did the teacher include standards from all five of the strands? How? Which standards did you identify embedded in her teaching?

3. How can you be intentional in incorporating multiple standards into your instruction?

Middle School Example

Over the course of several days, an eighth grade middle school class explores the mindset of several American revolutionaries by tracing these individuals' thinking before and during the American Revolution. The specific focus of the unit is *Students analyze how the events and dialogue in texts and primary sources reveal aspects of a character (in this case, a Revolutionary War figure), and then students utilize their analysis and research to write an argument in response to a guiding question based on that character's life, supporting their claims with clear reasons and relevant textual evidence.* This unit of study begins with the questions *What's worth fighting for in life? Why?* Students study the impact of these questions for identified American revolutionaries based on the events, people, and ideas of that period in history. A teacher and student-built text set that includes a variety of informational texts, historical fiction, video documentaries, and primary sources provides the necessary resources for the unit. Listed below are just a few examples of the multigenre, multileveled, and multimodal texts that were included in this text set:

- *Patriots in Boston* Reader's Theater (Teacher Created Materials)
- The Account of the Boston Massacre from Captain Thomas Preston, British Army
- The Boston Gazette and County Journal Account of the Boston Massacre, March 12, 1770
- "The Rich Lady Over the Sea," an authentic song from the Boston Tea Party time period, http://www.contemplator.com/america/richlady.html
- Map of Boston Harbor found at http://hdl.loc.gov/loc.pnp/cph.3c34241

- *Or Give Me Death: A Novel of Patrick Henry's Family* by Ann Rinaldi
- Excerpts from *The Declaration of Independence*
- *George vs. George: The American Revolution as Seen From Both Sides,* by Rosalyn Schanzer, 2004
- *Liberty! How the American Revolution Began,* by Lucille Recht, Penner, 2002

To introduce the unit, the teacher asks students the question *What's worth fighting for in life?* He spends a few minutes collecting student answers on a chart at the front of the room. (For example, some students might say *carrying cell phones, listening to music in class, civil rights, human rights.*) Then, he tells students that they will consider this question within a context from the past.

The teacher engages students in a close reading of Patrick Henry's speech, "Give Me Liberty or Give Me Death." He distributes copies of this speech to the students and tells them to follow along as they listen to an actor read this speech on YouTube®. After this first read, the teacher asks students to think about the most unusual or interesting thing said in the speech and to share their thoughts with those sitting nearby. Students talk to their groups a few minutes before the teacher gathers their attention and allows a few of them to share their thinking with the group. Based on the students' comments, the teacher asks some questions from the list below, being careful not to repeat or rehash what the students have already discussed.

- From this speech, we can conclude that the author is unhappy with how Great Britain has treated his country. What evidence supports this conclusion?
- What text evidence helps the reader understand the meaning of *subjugation* in paragraph four? What other words from this text need to be clarified for us to completely understand the message of the speech?
- What did Patrick Henry think was worth fighting for in his life? Why do you think that? What is your evidence?
- Explain the author's use of the symbol of a kiss in paragraph four. Is this effective? Why or why not?

The students discuss these questions and share their thinking with the group.

During a second session with the text, the teacher asks the students to search the speech for examples that show how the author employs different symbols. The students are also reminded to continue to dig into the meaning of the text. The teacher reads the text a second time as the students follow along in their own text. After this second read, the discussion continues with the teacher using following questions as a guide when needed to prompt students and probe their thinking. (Again, the teacher skips over topics that have already been discussed by students.)

- What other symbols does the author use? What could these symbols mean, and why do you think this? How does this symbol tie into the message of this speech?

- In what ways does the author persuade the listeners to his mindset? Point out examples from the text.

- Why would it be surprising to find out that this author had no formal education? Support your answers with references to the text.

- What kind of impact did this speech have on its listeners who wanted to go to war with Britain? Defend your answer with references to the text.

- At this time, Patrick Henry used words to fight for what he believed. Which is more effective, fighting with words or fighting with force? Why do you think so? Is that always true?

After the second discussion, the teacher divides the paragraphs of this speech among groups of students. (Paragraphs four and five are divided into two parts each to make them shorter.) The students select partners and take their assigned paragraphs, and practice a fluent reading of that text to each other while inferring, based on Henry's character and the events happening at the time, the tone in which Henry might have actually said that portion of the speech. Then, the teacher passes out an assortment of character trait cards with words such as *courageous, embittered, fearful, irate, convicted*. As the students select a trait card, they read their speech section with a voice that reflects that character trait and then discuss how that trait possibly detracts from or enhances the meaning of the text. The teacher identifies several student partnerships that might struggle a bit with the task and joins them for a short time to scaffold support as they begin the activity. He also monitors the students' progress by dropping in on small groups.

Finally the students debrief the above activity and how the various character trait cards impacted the delivery and meaning of Henry's speech. They discuss how they are able to infer from the speech's content how Henry would respond to the question *What is worth fighting for in your life?* The students watch a short biographical excerpt about Patrick Henry on YouTube® that explains how Henry, an uneducated person, learned to speak fluently by reading and practicing Shakespeare. They identify other events and experiences that impacted what he valued in his life.

In another class period, the students begin to examine the ideas and events surrounding other American revolutionaries. Students really dig into one of the identified individual's mind-set, motivations, and actions to infer what that character believed was worth fighting for in life. The students select one character from a list provided by the teacher. The list includes figures such as Samuel Adams, John Adams, Abigail Adams, Crispus Attucks, Molly Pitcher, Paul Revere, Benjamin Franklin, Benedict Arnold, and George Washington. The teacher reminds the students to focus their research about the individual they select on the answers to these key questions: *What was this individual's mindset during this time? What did this individual think was worth fighting for in his or her life? How did events, people, and/or ideas impact this individual's perspective?*

Students utilize a variety of texts from the available text set to research their American revolutionary. The teacher works with the content-area social studies teacher to provide students several class periods to research their selected character, using appropriate resources from the text set. During this time, the teacher conducts a series of modeled lessons on different aspects of research, such as:

- how to gather critical information from multiple sources and check source accuracy

- how to paraphrase text content during note taking to avoid plagiarism

- how to support your analysis of your individual with relevant, well-selected facts, quotations, concrete details, and examples

Both teachers meet with small groups based on what support different students need to proceed. The teachers also engage in quick individual conferences to observe students' progress and assess their effectiveness in collecting text evidence to construct a well-developed analysis that addresses the key questions.

When the students are ready to write about their American revolutionary, the teacher provides them with several differentiated choices for publishing their research. Students are told that their choice must meet the requirements by responding to the key questions completely and supporting all inferences/analysis with specific text evidence and sources. The students are also given a rubric by which each project will be evaluated. The teacher provides the students the following project options:

- Compose at least four diary entries written by your American revolutionary that reflects his/her mindset and responses to the key questions. Use *Diary of a Wimpy Kid* style diary entries as your model and include drawings/sketches with each entry.

- Create a social media page for your individual with critical comments/captions and accompanying "photos," graphics, etc., that show his or her mind-set and responses to the key questions reflected through his or her thoughts and interactions with others (Tumblr®, Facebook®, Twitter®, Instagram®, etc.).

- Develop a written script for a short documentary that describes your individual and his or her mindset and responses to the key questions. Use your phone or another video resource to record your documentary. You may choose to be the narrator, or you may ask other students to participate in different roles during the documentary based on your script (such as an interview or a commentary embedded in the documentary).

The students complete these projects over a two-day period. The teacher meets with each group based on the project they select, helps them analyze the task and review the assessment rubric for their project, and answers any questions. As the students work on their tasks, the teacher engages in quick individual conferences based on students' goals or needs. Once again, the content-area teacher steps in to work with the students on their projects during their history block.

For the culmination of the unit, the teacher stages the room like an exhibit hall, and the students rotate around the room to share their projects with their classmates. In addition, each student evaluates his or her own project and two other assigned students projects, using the rubrics provided. This activity takes up the entire class period. To sum up the experience, the students debrief in small discussion circles by sharing what they have learned about the events, people, and ideas of this time period and what these revolutionaries thought was worth fighting for in their lives.

In a follow-up session in the next day or two, the teacher brings the driving question forward to current day events by asking *What is worth fighting for in life today?* The teacher places students into groups and distributes several different newspapers and news magazines/online resources for students to peruse. Based on the content of the texts, the students generate a list of possible responses to this question, and they write their thoughts on a large piece of chart paper. Students explore the ideas and examine any connections between the topics. Students also discuss the different ways people fight for their ideas, beliefs, families, rights, etc. (examples: volunteering, giving speeches, staging protests, writing letters, boycotting, engaging in debates, running for office, enlisting in the military).

The teacher tells students that each of them will write a short argument essay responding to the following questions: *What is worth fighting for today? Why?* The students choose one of the topics reflected on the group chart, or they pick a different topic after pondering the key questions, discussing the questions with their family, or watching the news for additional ideas. Once students select their topic, they pose their argument in response to the question and read at least three texts to develop their claim and evidence.

After conducting their research, the students compose their individual short argument essays to present their claims supported by clear reasons and relevant text evidence. The teacher and students develop a rubric for assessment of the project. Students engage in an extended reader's/writer's workshop context over the course of several days so they can research their position using several texts, collect relevant text evidence for their claims, organize their arguments, draft their texts, revise their texts and meet with their writing partners, and edit their final copies. Since this is not the first argument text that the students have written, the teacher carefully monitors their progress and teaches several short modeled mini-lessons based on his assessment of need. He specifically returns to the organization of an argument text to make sure that the students present their reasons and claims logically. The teacher meets with small groups to briefly "dipstick" their progress and works with individual students who need extra support both in class and before or after school.

As a culmination to the writing experience, the students form triads to share their argument texts. They use their texts to defend their claims before their peers, and they respond to questions with relevant evidence from their written texts. They provide feedback and comments based on other students' work. The students are enthusiastic about sharing their arguments, and they have heartfelt conversations about their claims and evidence. The students turn in their argument texts along with a self-evaluation using the provided rubric.

1. How did the primary teaching focus develop throughout the unit?

2. This teacher had many other standards intentionally in play throughout the unit. Did the teacher include standards from the four strands and Literacy in History/Social Studies? How? Which standards did you identify that were embedded in his teaching?

3. How can you coordinate with subject-specific instructors to intentionally integrate multiple literacy standards into both ELA and content-area instruction?

Conclusion

As we have unwrapped the *what* of the CCSS to get to the critical *how*—the actual exemplary teaching needed to reach the vision of the standards—we hope that you have frequently paused and pondered the possibilities for your own classroom. We have explored together many ways that this *how* can look. None of the strategies or ideas presented are *the* way but are just some of many ways the *how* can evolve as we plan. This book just begins to touch on the potential that we all have within to make superb instructional decisions that ensure student success. We expect that you still have questions. So do we. But together as literacy experts and teachers who are dedicated to their students, we move forward together, remembering that *the most important questions don't seem to have ready answers. An answer is an invitation to stop thinking about something, to stop wondering . . . . An unanswered question is a fine traveling companion. It sharpens your eye for the road* (Remen 2006).

We will meet you on the road.

Let's Think and Discuss

1. Select any grade-level-specific standard. In what ways will integrating both reading and writing experiences meet multiple standards in your classroom?

2. What other specific ELA standards will be met in the process?

3. What kinds of support systems do you need to successfully implement these standards?

Teacher Resources

Consultant
Timothy Rasinski, Ph.D
Kent State University

Publishing Credits
Dona Herweck Rice, *Editor-in-Chief*
Lee Aucoin, *Creative Director*
Conni Medina, M.A.Ed., *Editorial Director*
Jamey Acosta, *Editor*
Robin Erickson, *Designer*
Stephanie Reid, *Photo Editor*
Rachelle Cracchiolo, M.S.Ed., *Publisher*

Image Credits
Cover Aziyka/Shutterstock; p.3 Monkey Business Images/Shutterstock;
p.4 RapidEye/istockphoto; p.5 kali9/istockphoto; p.6 4Gorilla/Shutterstock;
p.7 Anne Ackermann/Getty Images; p.8 Josef Muellek/dreamstime;
p.9 Blend Images/Shutterstock; p.10 Zurijeta/Shutterstock; p.11 lofoto/Shutterstock;
back cover Josef Muellek/dreamstime

Based on writing from *TIME For Kids*.

TIME For Kids and the *TIME For Kids* logo are registered trademarks of TIME Inc.
Used under license.

Teacher Created Materials
5301 Oceanus Drive
Huntington Beach, CA 92649-1030
http://www.tcmpub.com
ISBN 978-1-4333-3573-0
© 2012 by Teacher Created Materials, Inc.

2

Here we go!

3

We can go to a farm.

4

We can go to a beach.

5

We can go to a mountain.

6

We can go to a forest.

7

We can go to a zoo.

8

We can go to a store.

9

We can go many places.

10

We can go!

11

Words to Know

a	many
beach	mountain
can	places
farm	store
forest	to
go	we
here	zoo

12

References Cited

Adams, Marilyn Jager. *Beginning to Read: Thinking and Learning About Print.* Cambridge, MA: MIT Press, 1990.

Adler, Mary, Eija Rougle, Eileen Kaiser, and Samantha Caughlan. "Closing the Gap Between Concept and Practice: Toward More Dialogic Discussion in the Language Arts Classroom." *Journal of Adolescent & Adult Literacy* 47 (2004): 312–322.

Afflerbach, Peter, P. David Pearson, and Scott G. Paris. "Clarifying Differences Between Reading Skills and Reading Strategies." *The Reading Teacher* 61 (2008): 364–373.

Afflerbach, Peter, Byeong-Young Cho, Jong-Yun Kim, Maria Eliker Crassas, and Brie Doyle. "Reading: What Else Matters Besides Strategies and Skills?" *The Reading Teacher* 66 (2013): 440–448.

Allen, Janet. *Yellow Brick Roads: Shared and Guided Paths to Independent Reading 4–12.* Portland, ME: Stenhouse, 2000.

Allington, Richard L. "You Can't Learn Much from Books You Can't Read." *Educational Leadership* 60 (2001): 16–19.

———. "What I've Learned About Effective Reading Instruction from a Decade of Studying Exemplary Elementary Classroom Teachers." *Phi Delta Kappan* 83 (2002): 740–747.

———. "The Three Principles of Reading." Keynote, Event from the Council International Reading Association, Centennial, February 2003.

———. *What Really Matters for Struggling Readers: Designing Research-Based Programs.* Boston, MA: Pearson, 2006.

———. *What Really Matters for Struggling Readers: Designing Research-Based Programs (3rd Edition).* Boston, MA: Pearson, 2012.

————. "What Really Matters for Struggling Readers?" *The Reading Teacher* 66 (2013): 520–530.

Allington, Richard L. and Peter H. Johnston. "What Do We Know About Effective Fourth Grade Teachers and Their Classrooms?" 2001. http://www.albany.edu/cela/reports/allington/allington4thgrade13010.pdf

Allington, R. Rasinski, T., Heinemann. *Good-Bye Round Robin: 25 Effective Oral Reading Strategies*, Portsmouth, NH: Heinemann, 1998.

Anderson, Carl. *How's It Going?: A Practical Guide for Conferring with Student Writers*. Portsmouth, NH: Heinemann, 2000.

Anstey Michele, and Geoff Bull. *Teaching and Learning Multiliteracies: Changing Times, Changing Literacies*. Newark, DE: International Reading Association, 2006.

Au, Kathryn, Jacquelin H. Carroll, and Judith A. Scheu. *Balanced Literacy Instruction: A Teacher's Resource Book*. Norwood, MA: Christopher-Gordon, 1997.

Berk, Laura E., and Adam Winsler. "Vygotsky: His Life and Works" and "Vygotsky's Approach to Development." In *Scaffolding Children's Learning: Vygotsky and Early Childhood Learning*. Washington, DC: National Association for Education of Young Children, 1995.

Beyer, Barry K. *Practical Strategies for the Teaching of Thinking*. Boston, MA: Allyn & Bacon, 1987.

Bloom, Benjamin Samuel. *Taxonomy of Educational Objectives: The Classification of Educational Goals, Handbook I: Cognitive Domain*. New York: Longmans, Green, 1956.

Bodrova, Elena, and Deborah Leong. *Tools of the Mind: The Vygotskian Approach to Early Childhood Education*. Englewood Cliffs, NJ: Prentice-Hall, Inc., 1996.

Boushey, Gail and Joan Moser. *Daily Five: Fostering Literacy Independence in the Elementary Grades*. Portland, ME: Stenhouse, 2006.

Boyles, Nancy. "Closing in on Close Reading." *Educational Leadership* 70 (2012): 36–41.

Brinckloe, Julie. *Fireflies*. New York, NY: Simon and Schuster Children's Publishing Division, 1985.

Britton, James. "Writing and the Story of the World." In *Explorations in the Development of Writing, Theory, Research, and Practice*, edited by Barry M. Kroll and Gordon Wells, 3–30. New York, NY: Wiley, 1983.

Brown, S. and L. Kappes. *Implementing the Common Core State Standards: A Primer on "Close Reading of Text"* The Aspen Institute, October, 2012.

Burkins, Jan Miller, and Melody Croft. *Preventing Misguided Reading: New Strategies for Guided Reading Teachers*. Newark, DE: International Reading Association, 2010.

Calkins, Lucy, Mary Ehrenworth, and Christopher Lehman. *Pathways to the Common Core: Accelerating Achievement*. Portsmouth, NH: Heinemann, 2012.

Cambourne, Brian. "Toward An Educationally Relevant Theory of Literacy Learning: Twenty Years of Inquiry." *The Reading Teacher* 49 (1995): 182–190.

Cappiello and Dawes. Shell Education, Teaching with Text Sets, 2013

Clay, Marie. *Becoming Literate: The Construction of Inner Control*. Portsmouth, NH: Heinemann, 1991.

———. *Reading Recovery: A Guidebook for Teachers in Training*. Portsmouth, NH: Heinemann, 1993.

Coleman, David and Susan Pimentel. *Revised Publishers' Criteria for the Common Core State Standards in English Language Arts and Literacy, Grades 3–12*. Washington, DC: Council of Chief State School Officers. 2012. Retrieved from http://groups.ascd.org/resource/documents/122463-Publi shersCriteriaforLiteracyforGrades3-12.pdf

Conklin, Wendy. *Higher-Order Thinking Skills to Develop 21st Century Learners.* Huntington Beach, CA: *Shell Education*, 2012.

Conniff, Caroline. "How Young Readers Perceive Reading and Themselves as Readers." *English in Education*, 27 (1993): 19–25.

Darling-Hammond, Linda. *Teacher Quality and Student Achievement: A Review of State Policy Evidence.* Seattle, WA: Center for Teaching Policy, University of Washington, 1999.

Donnelley, Mark, and Julie Donnelley. *Guiding Adolescent Readers to Success.* Huntington Beach, CA: Shell Education, 2012.

Dorfman, Lynne R., and Rose Cappelli. *Mentor Texts: Teaching Writing through Children's Literature, K–6.* Portland, ME: Stenhouse Publishers, 2007.

Duffy, Gerald G. "Powerful Models or Powerful Teachers? An Argument for Teacher-As-Entrepreneur." In *Instructional Models in Reading*, edited by Steven A. Stahl and David A. Hayes, 351–365. Mahwah, NJ: Lawrence Earlbaum Associates, 1997.

Duke, Nell K., and P. David Pearson. "Effective Practice for Developing Reading Comprehension." In *What Research Has to Say About Reading Instruction (3rd Edition)*, edited by Alan E. Farstrup and S. Jay Samuels, 205–242. Newark, DE: International Reading Association, 2002.

Elder, Linda, and Richard Paul. "Critical Thinking: Why We Must Transform Our Teaching." *Journal of Developmental Education*, 18 (1994): 34–35.

Fisher, Douglas., and Frey, Nancy. *Better Learning Through Structured Teaching: A Framework for the Gradual Release of Responsibility (2nd Edition).* Alexandria, VA: ASCD, 2014

Fisher, Frey, and Lapp. "Close Reading in Elementary Schools," *The Reading Teacher* 66 (2012): 179–188.

Fountas, Irene, and Gay Su Pinnell. *Guided Reading: Good First Teaching for All Children.* Portsmouth, NH: Heinemann, 1996.

————. *Guiding Readers and Writers Grades 3–6: Teaching Comprehension, Genre, and Content Literacy.* Portsmouth, NH: Heinemann, 2001.

————. *The Continuum of Literacy Learning, Grades PreK-8, Second Edition: A Guide to Teaching.* Portsmouth, NH: Heinemann. 2010.

Freedman, Lauren. "The Way School Should Be: Navigating Learning with Text Sets." 2011. http://wowlit.org/blog/2011/05/02/the-way-school-should-be-navigating-learning-with-text-sets

Gambrell, Linda G., and Janice F. Almasi (Eds.). *Lively Discussions! Fostering Engaged Reading.* Newark, DE: International Reading Association, 1996.

Gambrell, Linda, Rose Marie Codling, and Barbara Martin Palmer. *Elementary Students' Motivation to Read.* Athens, GA: National Reading Research Center, 1996.

Gladis, Karie. Presentation on CCSS in English Language Arts. Huntington Beach, CA. 2013.

Graves, Donald. *A Fresh Look at Writing.* Portsmouth, NH: Heinemann, 1994.

Guthrie, John T., Allan Wigfield, and Wei You. *Instructional Contexts for Engagement and Achievement in Reading. Handbook of Research on Students Engagement,* edited by Sandra L. Christenson, Amy L. Reschly, and Cathy Wylie. New York: Springer, 2010.

Harvey, Stephanie, and Daniels, Harvey. *Comprehension and Collaboration: Inquiry Circles in Action.* Portsmouth, NH: Heinemann, 2009.

Harvey, Stephanie, and Anne Goudvis. *Strategies that Work: Teaching Comprehension to Enhance Understanding.* Portland, ME: Stenhouse Publishers, 2000, 2007.

Hill, Susan. *Guiding Literacy Learners.* Portland, ME: Stenhouse Publishers, 1999.

Holdaway, D. *The Foundations of Literacy.* Sydney, Australia: Ashton Scholastic, 1979.

Ivey, Gay. "Getting Started: Manageable Literacy Practices." *Educational Leadership* 60 (2002): 20–23.

Jensen, Eric P. *Brain-Based Learning: The New Science of Teaching and Training.* San Diego, CA: The Brain Store, 2000.

Johnston, Peter. *Choice Words: How Our Language Affects Children's Learning.* Portland, ME: Stenhouse, 2004.

Kasten, Wendy C., Janice V. Kristo, and Amy A. McClure. *Living Literature*: *Using Children's Literature to Support Reading and Language Arts.* Columbus, OH: Merrill/Prentice Hall, 2005.

Kasten, Wendy C., and Lori G. Wilfong. "Encouraging Independent Reading with Ambience: The Book Bistro in Middle and Secondary School Classes." *Journal of Adolescent & Adult Literacy* 48 (2005): 656–664.

Lobel, Arnold. *Frog and Toad Are Friends.* New York, NY: HarperCollins, 2003.

Lyons, Carol. *Teaching Struggling Readers: How to Use Brain-Based Research to Maximize Learning.* Portsmouth, NH: Heinemann, 2003.

Manning, Gary L., and Manning, Maryann. "What Models of Recreational Reading Make a Difference?" *Reading World* 23 (1984): 375–380.

Marzano, Robert J. *The Art and Science of Teaching: A Comprehensive Framework for Effective Instruction.* Alexandria, VA: Association for Supervision and Curriculum Development, 2007.

Marzano, Robert J., and John S. Kendall. *Content Knowledge: A Compendium of Standards and Benchmarks for K–12 Education.* Aurora, CO: Mid-Continent Regional Educational Laboratory, 2000.

McGee, Lea. "Talking About Books with Young Children." In *Book Talk and Beyond: Teachers Respond to Literature,* edited by Nancy Roser and Miriam Martinez, Newark, DE: International Reading Association, 1995.

Murphy, Debby. *You Can't Just Say It Louder!: Differentiated Strategies for Comprehending Nonfiction.* Huntington Beach, CA: Shell Education, 2010.

National Governors Association Center for Best Practices, Council of Chief State School Officers. 2010. *Common Core State Standards: English Language Arts Standards.* Washington, DC: National Governors Association Center for Best Practices, Council of Chief State School Officers.

Nichols, Maria. *Talking About Text: Guiding Students to Increase Comprehension through Purposeful Talk.* Huntington Beach, CA: Shell Education, 2009.

O'Connor-Stockton, Kimberly. Presentation on CCSS in English Language Arts. Huntington Beach, CA, 2013.

Opitz, Michael F., and Timothy Rasinski. *Good-Bye Round Robin: 25 Effective Oral Reading Strategies.* Portsmouth, NH: Heinemann, 1998.

Partnership for Assessment of Readiness for College and Careers. "PARCC Model Content Frameworks: English Language Arts/ Literacy Grades 3–11." 2011. www.parcconline.org/sites/parcc/files/ PARCCMCFELALiteracyAugust2012_FINAL.pdf

Pearson, P. David. "Reclaiming the Center." In *The First R: Every Child's Right to Read*, edited by Michael Graves, Paul van den Broek, and Barbara M. Taylor, 259–274. New York: Teachers College Press, 1996.

———. "The Influence of Reading Recovery on Everyday Classroom Practice." Presentation, Presented at the fifth International Reading Recovery Conference, New Zealand, 2004.

Pearson, P. David, and Linda Fielding. "Comprehension Instruction." In *Handbook of Reading Research, Volume Two,* edited by Rebecca Barr, Michael L. Kamil, Peter B. Mosenthal, and P. David Pearson, 815–860. White Plains, NY: Longman, 1991.

Pearson, P. David, and Margaret C. Gallager. "The Instruction of Reading Comprehension." *Contemporary Educational Psychology* 8 (1983): 317–344.

Popham, W. James. "The Lowdown on Learning Progressions." 2007. http://mathcurriculumreview.pbworks.com/w/file/fetch/67005847/Popham_2007.pdf

Remen, Rachel Naomi. *Kitchen Table Wisdom*. New York, NY: Berkley Publishing Group, 2006.

Reutzel, D., Jones, C.D., and Newman, T.H. Scaffolded Silent Reading: Improving the Conditions of Silent Reading Practice in Classrooms. In E.H. Hiebert, & D. Reutzel (Eds.), Revisiting Silent Reading, 129-150). Newark, DE: International Reading Association, 2010.

Routman, Regie. *Reading Essentials: The Specifics You Need to Teach Reading Well*. Portsmouth, NH: Heinemann, 2003.

Sanden, Sherry. "Independent Reading: Perspectives and Practices of Highly Effective Teachers." *The Reading Teacher* 66 (2012): 222–231.

Serravallo, Jennifer. *Teaching Reading in Small Groups: Differentiated Instruction for Building Strategic, Independent Readers*. Portsmouth, NH: Heinemann, 2010.

Shapiro, Jon, and William White. "Reading Attitudes and Perceptions in Traditional and Nontraditional Reading Programs." *Reading Research and Instruction*, 30 (1991): 52–66.

Stiggins, Rick J., Judith A. Arter, Jan Chappuis, and Steve Chappuis. *Classroom Assessment for Student Learning: Doing It Right—Using It Well*. Portland, OR: Assessment Training Institute, Inc., 2004.

Tharp, Roland G., and Ronald Gallimore. *Rousing Minds to Life: Teaching Learning, and Schooling in Social Context*. New York, NY: Cambridge University Press, 1988.

Tomlinson, Carol A., and Jay McTighe. *Integrating Differentiated Instruction and Understanding by Design: Connecting Content and Kids*. Alexandria VA: ASCD, 2006.

Tovani, Cris. *Do I Really Have to Teach Reading?* Portland, ME: Stenhouse Publishers, 2004.

Van Nostrand, A. D. "Writing and the Generation of Knowledge." *Social Education* (1979): 178–180.

Vygotsky, Lev S. *Thought and Language.* Cambridge, MA: MIT Press, 1962.

Webb, Norman. Webb's Depth of Knowledge Guide: Career and Technical Definitions. http://www.aps.edu/rda/documents/resources/Webbs_DOK_ Guide.pdf (accessed August 12, 2013), 2009.

Wilhelm, Jeffrey D. *Improving Comprehension with Think-Aloud Strategies: Modeling What Good Readers Do.* New York, NY: Scholastic, 2001.

Wood, David, Jerome S. Bruner, and Gail Ross. "The Role of Tutoring in Problem Solving." *Journal of Child Psychology and Psychiatry* 17 (1976): 89–100.

Zwiers, J. and M. Crawford. *Academic Conversations: Classroom Talk That Fosters Critical Thinking and Content Understandings.* Portland, ME, Stenhouse Publishers, 2011.